Dear Cloudsifter,

Thank you for blessing
my life. May your
mission unfold with
power and love.

Lotsa Love and Light
Wally

THE RESULTS BOOK

How to flow with the universe
and eliminate the frustrations in your life

Wally Minto

Printed by
Hawkes Publishing Inc.
P.O. Box 65735
Salt Lake City, Utah 84107

A NOTE FROM THE AUTHOR

I did not create this Results Book nor do I claim any credit for its development. This Results Book is like an intelligent, individual entity which began and has grown from its own intelligence. It might be likened unto a tree which begins from its own seed and grows through its own intelligence. The tree expresses its growth through its environment, through the soil, water, sun and air. However, this environment does not give the tree the intelligence to grow. It grows because of its own intelligence through this environment.

Because of my individual experience in life, I developed certain personality traits and belief systems that caused me to become a fertile environment for the beginning and the growth of this Results Book. In other words, I did not create the Results Book, it has simply been expressed through me and many of the ideas expressed were completely foreign to me when I first became aware of them.

I am sure that if this Results Book had not been expressed through me that it would have found another person who was a fertile environment for its expression and this book would exist today whether or not I existed.

TABLE OF CONTENTS

8

The balance of life...is something missing?

You are spiritual, mental and physical being human

Your unconscious mind is most powerful

Ego in the physical dimension is perfect

You have a perfect spiritual space, mental space and physical space

All creation already is

Result ◄——————— Effect ◄——————— Cause

How to change your act into an answer

What you are, what you do, what you have is perfect

Learn to act without decisions

How to free yourself without judgment

The truth shall set you free--The truth is

The following public classes are taught by the author, Wally Minto: Alpha Awareness Training, Results Training, De-Stress Seminar, Post Graduate Training Seminar. Alpha Awareness Training and Results Training are also available on cassette tapes from one of Wally's actual class presentations.

You may order the RESULTS BOOK ($8.)
The ALPHA AWARENESS TRAINING BOOK ($13)
and cassette tapes from
Alpha Awareness
Drawer G
Susanville, CA 96130
Order forms on page 172

PART I

I would like to extend to you a warm welcome into this RESULTS BOOK on "How to Flow with the Universe and Eliminate the Frustrations in Your Life." Now that you have paid your twelve dollars for the book we can go ahead and get started. I would like to caution you though, for if you read through this book looking for twelve dollars of value you may never finish reading it. For your benefit I wish I could have charged you ten thousand dollars for this book, but I am sure if I had, I would be the only one reading it.

 The reason this is a $10,000 book is because it is in no way designed to give you any more knowledge but rather to help you understand and gain enlightenment from the knowledge you already have. You probably know an individual who has his cranium crammed full of knowledge without an ounce of understanding or enlightenment to go with it, and if you do, it may be apparent that all the knowledge in the world without understanding or enlightenment is pretty useless. So instead of seeking more knowledge as you read this book, use it to understand the knowledge you already have. Read this book to give yourself enlightenment. If you are wondering what enlightenment really is, enlightenment is the ah-hahs you experience in life. When you are doing something and suddenly you say, "Ah-hah, now I understand," that's enlightenment.

You will receive more ah-hahs from this book if you are aware that you have probably already flowed with the universe in being a professional mind wanderer. So let's take a moment to understand mind wandering, what causes it, what are the effects of it, and then how we might control it. First of all, do you mentally talk to yourself? .... You might answer as most people do, "Some of the time." But the reality is you mentally talk to yourself, either through subvocalization or the process of thinking, every minute of your waking state. In fact, while you are reading these words, you are mentally talking to yourself.

The problem of mind wandering is not caused by simply talking to yourself but by the fact that you are talking to yourself faster than you are reading these words. If someone is talking to you, you are usually talking to yourself at least four times faster. That may seem awfully impolite but we all do it, and I many times wonder what other people are talking about while I'm talking to them. To put this in a comparison, let's say the words coming from someone talking to you is a car speeding along the highway at 100 miles per hour. Your self-talk then is a jet airplane traveling at 400 miles per hour. Now, how might you keep the two of them together without the jet leaving the car? Usually someone suggests slowing the jet down but this won't work because it is nearly impossible to slow down your self-talk. So why not have the jet circling at 400 miles per hour over the car traveling at 100 miles per hour and now the two of them can stay together.

Hopefully now you are beginning to get a little bit of

an ah-hah because this is part of the answer to controlling mind wandering. How many times have you been reading a book and at the end of the chapter you realized you didn't even know what you had been reading, or you listened to an hour lecture and didn't have any idea what it was about, or you've just been introduced to someone and ten seconds later you couldn't remember their name. This happened because your self-talk went off 400 miles an hour in a different direction.

If you want to tremendously improve your recall and control your mind wandering, then simply talk to yourself about whatever you want your mind to focus on. As you are reading this book, talk to yourself about each paragraph as you are reading it. Constantly ask yourself questions about the material and listen to your answers as you are reading. If, like the jet, you circle with the material as you are reading it, when you've finished the book you will know what it is about. That is, if you avoid the second problem caused by this mind wandering self-talk. Most people tend to use their self-talk to instantly accept or reject whatever they are perceiving. In other words, they instantly decide to believe or disbelieve, like or dislike, whatever they see, hear, touch, taste, or smell. Usually when you reject information it does not make a strong brain cell impression and tends to become the so-called forgotten information. If you are reading a textbook and you reject every other paragraph or chapter, when the final exam comes you only have one-half of the information impressed on brain cells for easy recall, and this usually results in a "D" rather than an "A" on the test.

Many times an idea you have rejected in the beginning will relate to another idea later on in a book and if you have rejected the first idea, the second idea will not make any sense either. If you don't understand an idea, don't reject it. Many times later on, a related idea will cause it to make sense. This does not mean you should accept every idea as you are reading a book. It simply means putting it all together by reading the whole book, then with the total book in mind you are free to accept or reject whatever parts you desire. Now if you will be aware of these two control factors of mind wandering, I'm sure you will receive many personal ah-hahs as you are reading this book. In other words, self-talk about the ideas you are reading. Like the jet airplane, circle with the material, and don't accept or reject the ideas until you have finished reading the whole book.

To help you experience more ah-hahs as you read this book, understand there may be ideas and concepts presented that you may resist because this book is about flowing through life without frustration and effort. However, your brain may be programmed that living is filled with frustration and it takes a lot of effort to fail in life, let alone succeed.

To help you overcome this possible resistance, read this book with this perspective in mind: in perceiving and using the value of this book, it does not matter if you believe or disbelieve the concepts; it doesn't matter if the concepts are true or untrue; it does not matter if these concepts are right or wrong. It's rather like being in a period of deep depression. If you pretend or act like you are happy, what is the result? If you pretend or act like you are happy, the result is that you're going to experience more happiness. However, it is not true to say that you are happy when you are depressed. If you are depressed, you're depressed, you are not happy. It is not true to say that you are happy, yet the result is, if you pretend or act like you are happy, you will actually experience more happiness. So keep the perspective in mind as you read this book; it doesn't really matter whether it's true or not true; it doesn't matter if you believe it or don't believe it. It simply means that you can use the concepts of this book to bring greater happiness, peace of mind, and success into your life without concerning yourself about belief or disbelief.

Every now and then someone will ask me: "Wally, do you really believe all these things you are saying?" My very honest answer is: "I don't know." I have never spent much time in believing or disbelieving these concepts; I simply use them. In using them I bring more joy and peace, more happiness and success, more of the things I desire, into each day of my life. I encourage you to use this same perspective. Don't concern yourself with believing or disbelieving this material but simply use those parts of it which can bring more happiness into your life.

The first thing to become aware of is how we human beings usually become something. Let's say a little girl, ten or twelve years old, wants to become a singer. What are some of the things that must happen for this girl to become a singer? We perhaps might all agree that she must have a good voice. She must have desire. She must have ability. She must have teachers. She must have money. She must have the proper wardrobe, and so on.

Now isn't it interesting to note that the entire list we have made up are all things this little girl must **have** before she can become a singer. This is where we usually start in life when we are going to become something, by first gathering together all of the things we must have. We always seem to start out in an area of **having**.

Now, once the little girl does have the desire, the voice, the teacher, the wardrobe, the money, then what must happen next for her to become a singer? She must start training her voice, learning new songs, learning the poise and the grace and the posture required. In other words, she starts doing what singers do. And so the second step human beings go through to become something is the process of doing. We go from **having** to **doing**. HAVE —▶ DO

Now once she has completed the process of doing-- she has perfected her voice, learned many different songs, learned perfect poise and posture--then what must happen next for her to become a singer? ... So that we might zero in on the correct answer, let's imagine this girl now sixteen or seventeen years old giving her first performance in public. She sings several songs with perfect poise and posture, perfect tone and quality. Has she now become a singer? You're probably inclined to answer yes, but what if the entire audience stands up and leaves the room without applauding, has she become a singer? No! If at the end of her performance though, the audience gives her applause and a standing ovation, has she then become a singer? Yes. You see, before the girl can be a singer, other people must agree that she is a singer. And so we go from the process of **doing** into that of **being** by the agreement of other people. This is the way nearly everybody becomes something. HAVE→DO→BE. We start by gathering together all the things that we must have. If we are fortunate to have enough then we can start doing; we start learning and practicing. And then, finally, if we can get enough agreement from other people, we end up being. Isn't this true?

I mean we all know that if you're ever going to be rich, first you must have money. So we start by scrimping and saving and putting money in the bank. We go without vacations and many of the little things we would like to have, until finally we have enough money and we can start doing what rich people do. We can invest in the stock market or buy a little real estate. When we have been doing what rich people do long enough, then other people will agree that we are rich. Once we have become rich through the agreement of other people, then it seems like everyone helps us become richer. Isn't it true the rich person usually gets the biggest discount? People are always offering to do little favors for someone they consider to be rich. If two people go out for dinner, one who is very rich and one who is very poor, who usually pays for the meal? Isn't it usually the poorest one who always grabs for the check first? The reason he reaches for the check is because he is striving to get other people to agree that he is rich. We know that if other people think we are rich, then money is easier to come by.

Now it is O.K. to go from having to doing to being because a lot of people have become rich and a lot of people have become singers in this manner, so there is proof that it works. The unfortunate thing is that the whole universe naturally, normally flows in the opposite direction. The universe flows from **being** into **doing** into **having. HAVE◄–DO◄–BE**.The reason we have struggled so hard all of our lives is because we have been going against the flow of the universe. We have been going from **having** into **doing** into **being.** If we will turn around and flow with the universe from **being** into **doing** into **having,** we eliminate all of the frustration and effort.

You cannot stop or change the direction of the flow of the universe. Even when you are going against the universe, it still carries you along with its flow. The universe might be compared to a river flowing along at ten miles per hour. Going against the flow of the universe is like swimming two miles an hour upstream against the current of the river. The current of the river is still carrying you along with it. By struggling against the current you are putting forth a lot of effort and only slowing yourself down to eight miles per hour. When you are swimming against the current you can never see where you are going because the current is carrying you backwards at eight miles per hour. Consequently, you are bound to hit a few unexpected rocks and rapids or rough places. If you are flowing with the current, you can see where you are going and you have the freedom to avoid the rocks and rough places. You can even stop swimming, and just float along pleasantly relaxed letting the current carry you.

When your life is flowing with the universe there is no struggle. When you seem to be fighting life and you are constantly seeing things to criticize and condemn, you are going against the flow of the universe. When your life doesn't seem to have a direction, you are going from having to doing to being. When you let your life flow with the current, you always have a natural direction.

Once in a while we see a person who naturally flows with the universe. We ask a little seven-or eight-year-old girl, "What are you going to be when you grow up?", and she answers, "I'm a singer." And in her little bare feet and tattered and torn dress, without any wardrobe, any poise or balance, without any singing voice or ability, without having any of the things we said she had to have, she sings us a song, and she is being a singer. Then when she's twelve or thirteen again someone asks, "What are you going to be when you grow up?", and she says, "I'm a singer." And again, without having any of these things we said she had to have, she sings a song for us and she is still **being** a singer. Then when she is seventeen or eighteen, someone hears her singing, and they say, "Wow! She is a singer! Let's start training her." So she starts **doing** what singers do. She starts training her voice, learning new songs, new routines, and she ends up **having** all of the things singers have--all the recognition, the audiences, the money, the wardrobe, the costumes. You see, this child was **being** a singer all of her life. Therefore, she never needed the agreement of other people to become a singer. Isn't it true, there have been famous singers who didn't even have a good voice. Now, you can become anything going in either direction, against the flow of the universe or flowing with it. It's simply that it takes less effort if you flow with the universe from **being** into **doing** into **having.**

Everyone has flowed with the universe at different times in different ways by starting out in being. Haven't you gotten up some morning just just **being** depressed? You didn't **have** anything to be depressed about, you were simply being depressed. Now when you got up just **being** depressed, did it take any effort to start **doing** what depressed people do--feeling sorry for yourself, thinking about all of the things in your life that are not going the way you want them to, and then **having** all the misery and sorrow that a depressed person has? Think of how much effort it would take if you got up one morning and you said to yourself, "What shall I **be** today?" And then you decided, "I think I'll **be** depressed." Now first you must have something to be depressed about. So you think about all the debts you have or you start a quarrel with your husband or wife so now you **have** something to be depressed about. Then you start **doing** what depressed people do. You start feeling sorry for yourself because you are in debt or because you are angry and finally you end up **being** depressed. Wouldn't it take a lot more effort to become depressed in that manner than to flow with the universe and simply start out **being** depressed when you get up?

Yet this is the way most people become rich or successful or happy or anything else. Most people believe that if they are going to **be** happy, they must **have** something to be happy about. But if you will flow with the universe from **being** into **doing** into **having** and start out just **being** happy, then you end up **having** all of the things that result from happiness.

Some of you reading this book may find it difficult to

identify with this concept. This is possibly because you have some background in positive thinking, goal structuring, metaphysics, psychocybernetics, or some related area, because all of these teachings tell you that you don't have to **have** money to become rich. You simply start out in the area of **doing,** thinking like a rich person, acting like a rich person, talking like a rich person, **doing** what rich people do, and eventually that will cause you to become rich. Isn't that the main theory of positive thinking or that type of an approach? Those people who are really using positive thinking, metaphysics, psychocybernetics, or some related teaching, have taken a gigantic step toward becoming anything they desire to be because they have eliminated the first hurdle that most people never get across--that of gathering together all of the things that you must **have** before you can even begin **doing** anything about **becoming** something. However, even with positive thinking and all of its related areas, you still must go against the flow of the universe from **doing** into **being.**

Now the reason positive thinking approaches haven't been working for you all of the time is because even though consciously you are starting out in the area of **doing,** subconsciously you are still hanging onto **having.** I know this may be hard for you to identify with, because consciously you believe that you do not need to start out **having** money to become rich, but subconsciously you believe that you are what you have. You see, if someone parked your car in the middle of the street, and then had two big bulldozers lower their blades and come together on each end of your car and crush it, what would happen to a little bit of you? A little bit of you would be crushed too, wouldn't it? Or if someone poured gasoline all the way around the foundation of your home and touched a match to it and you watched your home and everything you have in it go up in flames, what would happen to a little bit of you? A little bit of you would be going up in flames too, wouldn't it? You see, subconsciously you are still clinging to the programming that you are what you have and that is why your positive thinking is not working for you all the time.

The reason most people start out in **having** is because then they can get agreement in **doing** and **being.** Those of you who have studied in the areas of positive thinking sometimes drop your friends who are not willing to study in those same areas because they will not agree with you. They will not agree that you can become rich by just **doing** what rich people do. It's for this same reason that we find it difficult to start out being because we're afraid that people will tell us we are wrong. Let's say you start out tomorrow just being rich, being a millionaire, as you will find out you really can by the time you finish this book. Then you meet a friend who wants to know what you're so happy about. And you say, "I'm happy because I'm rich." So your friend says, "That's great, then you can pay   back the twenty dollars I loaned you last week." And you say to your friend, "I can't pay you back the money because I don't have any money, I'm just being rich." What's your friend going to say to you? He's going to say, "You're crazy, you are wrong." So the reason we seldom start out being is because of a programmed fear of **being wrong.** We tend to reject anything that makes us wrong.

If we want a nice big tomato and instead somebody hands us a little tomato seed, we have the tendency to say, "But that's wrong. That's not right because I asked for a tomato." But isn't the perfection of the tomato within the tomato seed? Maybe later on somebody hands us a little tomato plant. We still have the tendency to say, "That's wrong. That's not right because I asked for a tomato." Yet isn't the perfection of the tomato still within the little tomato plant? Even when someone hands us a full-grown tomato plant, we still say, "That's wrong. That's not right because I asked for a tomato." But you see, the perfection of the tomato is still within the full-grown plant. Even as the perfection of the tomato is within every tomato seed and every tomato plant, so is the perfection of the inner-self within every human being. You see, the difference between man and the tomato plant is that man has ego, which is that part of his conscious personality which compares himself to his reality, and because the tomato plant has no ego, the only thing it will do to the best of its ability is to express the perfection of the tomato within. In other words, the little tomato plant doesn't look up at the great big tomato plant and say, "There must be something wrong with me because he's bigger than I am." And the great big tomato plant doesn't look down at the little tiny tomato plant and say, "There must be something wrong with you, because you're not as big as me." The difference between man and the tomato plant is that man has ego, which he uses for comparison and judgment and so to be aware of perfection is also to be aware of imperfection, as to be aware of success is to be aware of failure. To be aware of happiness is to be aware of depression. To be aware of living is to be aware of dying.

So we have man, who was created in the image in perfection, and since man seemed to be innately aware of that inner perfection, he then felt he had to have a guideline so that he could tell if he was expressing his inner perfection or imperfection. Unfortunately much of that guideline became the concept of right and wrong. Man began saying, "If I am being right, I am expressing my perfection, but if I am being wrong, I am expressing my imperfection." Now this guideline may be O.K. for many things, but as a guideline for expressing inner perfection it is a fallacy. You see, for every right that you can give me in the world, I can give you a whole society that will call that right, wrong. And for every wrong you can give me in the world, I can give you a whole society that will tell you that that wrong is right. Now if we have a minus one and a plus one and we put the two together, what do we end up with? Nothing, they cancel each other out, and if every right is also wrong and every wrong also right, then they cancel each other out. Right and wrong are predominantly based on the agreement or disagreement of other people. Understand, if you went out and murdered somebody tonight and everybody agreed with you, you would be doing the right thing.

Can you understand now why you may resist some of the concepts in this book? Because, you see, a large majority of your brain cell impressions are probably based on right and wrong, and in using this concept, right and wrong are a fallacy as a guideline for the expression of your inner perfection. Now please don't let your belief systems get in your way and stop you from using the value of this concept before you understand it. You will receive more ah-hahs from this book if you will put your belief systems aside and neither accept nor reject the ideas until you've finished the book. If you don't, you may say things like: "With the problem 2+2, the right answer is 4." It might better be said that 4 is the correct answer. In our concept we are not concerned with correct or incorrect but rather with right and wrong, in terms of judgment.

If you hang onto your belief systems you may say, "The Bible says it is wrong to kill." Or, "It is wrong to hate your enemy." More so than right or wrong, the Bible simply and beautifully teaches doing and not doing. "Thou shalt not kill. Thou shalt love thine enemy."

The Bible does teach: "Judge not, lest ye be judged." Since we were small children we have understood that message. At a very early age we realized that every time we judged we were judged in return and nearly every time the judgment we received was more than the judgment we put out. When we told one of our playmates he was stupid, he never answered back saying, "You're right. I'm stupid and you're a genius." No. Instead he always came back with something like, "Well, you are so dumb and stupid, you're an idiot." And so we always got back more judgment than we put out which creates the strongest fear in the human race, the fear of being wrong.

The fear of being criticized, condemned, or called wrong by someone else is one of the strongest fears in the human race. Probably more failures have been caused by the fear of being wrong than by all the rest of the causes put together.

How many times in your life have you found it difficult to do something because you were afraid you might do it the wrong way? Have you found it difficult to speak in front of a small group because you thought you might forget what you were going to say? Have you found it difficult to learn some sport like skiing because you were afraid you might do the wrong thing, like fall down? How many times have you experienced unnecessary stress when taking a test because you were afraid you might put down the wrong answer? How many times in your youth did you do something that you didn't want to do and knew you shouldn't do but you knew the group of kids you were with would make you wrong if you didn't? How many times in just the last few weeks have you found it difficult to communicate with your husband or wife, parents or children, boyfriend or girlfriend, boss, employee, or one of your friends, or even a stranger because you were afraid the other person might think you were wrong? The fear of being wrong, the fear of not being right, is one of the strongest fears in the human race. Perhaps more failures have been caused, more dreams and goals have never been reached, more friendships have been destroyed, more marriages broken up, because of the fear of being wrong than for all the other causes put together. "Judge not, lest ye be judged." Whenever you call someone else wrong, you must realize that it does not make you right. Instead, in the other person's mind you also become wrong. Therefore, the more you call other people wrong, the more inhibited you become through the fear of being wrong.

You think when you agree with something that makes it right and when you disagree with something that makes it wrong. That is your illusion because the only thing you can make right or wrong is yourself. The only thing you can judge is your experience and your experience is you and not the thing you are judging.

You may judge this book to be interesting or boring. The illusion is that you think the book is interesting or boring. The reality is that you have judged your experience of the book to be interesting or boring and as your experience is you, the ultimate reality is that you have judged yourself to be interested or bored.

Let's look at the way two different people might judge their experience of a rainy day. One person looks at the rain and says, "It's another rotten lousy rainy day." The farmer looks at the rain and says, "Thank God, it's raining. It's beautiful, it's fantastic." Their judgment then produces a specific brain chemistry causing them to feel rotten and lousy or beautiful and fantastic. Their illusion is they think the rain caused them to feel rotten and lousy or beautiful and fantastic. The reality is it was their judgment of their experience that caused them to feel lousy or fantastic. Rain is not rotten or lousy or beautiful or fantastic. Rain is simply rain. You may experience it in any way you choose to.

When you call something or someone, including yourself, wrong, it causes you to feel some degree of negative emotion. It will cause some degree of fear, worry, guilt, anger, resentment, frustration, or tension, and these negative emotions cause your body to release toxins into your system. These toxins are poison to your system and so some element within the body has to be used to neutralize the poison, which creates an imbalance in your body chemistry.

This process that goes on within your mind and body is very similar to a court case. If you are found wrong or guilty in court, then the judge passes a sentence upon you, the sentence is your punishment so that you will suffer for your wrongness. When you judge something to be wrong which is literally calling yourself or your experience wrong, it will usually cause some degree of negative emotion. The negative emotion causes your body to release toxins into your system. This causes an imbalance in your body chemistry which can cause illness. So whenever you call something wrong, your punishment is to literally take a little bit of poison and enough poison can certainly make you ill. If you constantly judge things to be wrong, over a period of time it may put so much poison into your system that it might even kill you.

Realize that whenever you call someone else wrong, you are really only calling your experience of them wrong and, therefore, the more you call other people wrong, the more inhibited you become through the fear of being wrong.

Understand that **being** right simply means receiving agreement from other people. And because the majority of your brain cell patterns are based on right and wrong this means that nearly everything you are, and nearly everything you do, and nearly everything you have, you are that, you do that, and you have that because it makes you right. Let's circle with that again. Nearly everything you are, everything you do, and everything you have, you are that, you do that, and you have that because it makes you right.

If you are a lousy housekeeper, and you know you are a lousy housekeeper, and all of your friends know you are a lousy housekeeper, and especially your husband knows you are a lousy housekeeper, what must you be to be right? You must be a lousy housekeeper. What do you suppose the husband would say if he came home from work one evening and the house was spotless--everything was picked up, swept, dusted, mopped--the house was in perfect order? What would he say? He would say, "What's wrong with you?" Well, husbands, you had better tune in because she's not going to be wrong, and she will keep a dirty house for the rest of her life so that she can be right.

If we have a teenager who is lazy, and he knows he's lazy, and mom and dad know he's lazy, and all of his brothers and sisters know he's lazy, what must the teenager be to be right? Yes, he must be lazy. If the teenager cleaned the garage or mowed the lawn, or cleaned the yard without anybody telling him to, what do you suppose his parents would say to him? "What's wrong with you?"

If you are always ill, and you know you are always ill, and your family knows you are always ill, and your doctor knows you're always ill, what must you be to be right? Yes, you must be ill. If a child is stupid; everything he does is stupid. What must the child be to be right? He must go through life being stupid.

Those of you who are parents, open up your awareness. If a child is always wrong; if he is always hearing statements like, "Can't you ever do anything right? Every time you do something, it's wrong," then what must the child be to be right, to receive agreement from other people? He must be wrong. And the child goes through life receiving agreement from all of his family and all of his friends by always doing the wrong thing. What do you suppose the father would say if the child did something and it turned out to be right? Sure, he would say, "What's wrong with you today, you did the right thing."

You see, human beings would rather go through life **being right doing the wrong thing** than to go through life **being wrong doing the right thing.** Let's circle with that again. You would rather be right and do the wrong thing than be wrong and do the right thing.

So, as we go through life we get into the habit of doing the right thing. We go through life acting the way other people agree we should act, and these acts or habits become what might be called comfort zones. Habits are comfort zones because in all the misery caused by our habits, we are comfortable. By comfort zones, I mean anything we have become accustomed to being, doing, or having. For instance, you all have comfort zones in the type of wardrobe you have. All of your clothes are pretty much the same type or style. You all have comfort zones in the kind of friends you associate with. The amount of income you make each year is a comfort zone. If you wives really want to know what a comfort zone is, go to bed before your husband does tonight and go to sleep on his side of the bed. What's going to happen when he comes to bed? I'm sure he will move you over so he can sleep on **his** side. Is the bed any softer on his side? No! It's simply because that's his comfort zone.

Do you sit at the same place at the table meal after meal in your home? Does the food taste any better there? Yes, it really does. When you are sitting in the wrong place, food doesn't taste as good. This is why you make your company so uncomfortable when you invite them over for dinner and they ask you where you want them to sit and you say, "Any place." And they just stand there. Do you understand why? They don't want to take your comfort zone because when they invite you over for dinner, they don't want you to take their comfort zone. If you would tell them where the kids usually sit and let them take one of their places, they would be more comfortable. We know the kids are not so set in their comfort zones so we don't mind taking them away.

You've probably seen a family whose comfort zone is a run-down home with paint peeling off, a couple of windows broken, the screen kicked out of the screen door, the lawn is dead, and the shrubbery is dying, and there are two or three junkers in the front yard. Finally, they decide to change it. They go out into the suburbs and buy a beautiful new home, all landscaped, with a new lawn, beautiful shrubbery, and what does it look like a year later? The lawn is dead, the shrubbery's dying out, two or three junkers in the front yard, and the screen is kicked out. They are right back in their same comfort zone.

Haven't you seen it again and again? This has been proven in the world of business. A company has a salesman who is in a fifty thousand dollar territory making seventy thousand dollars a year. So they move him into a ninety thousand dollar territory so that he can really make a good income. How much money does he make that year! His same seventy thousand, because that's his comfort zone. Even though a seventy thousand dollar income may be a tremendous problem because he really needs ninety thousand to live on, he still clings to his seventy thousand dollar comfort zone.

Can you understand now why it is so difficult to change your habits, your comfort zones? It is because nearly all of your brain cell patterns are based on right and wrong. You see, if you change your comfort zone, you are admitting that something must have been wrong with it or there would be no reason to change it, would there? If you change jobs, what do people ask you? "What was wrong with the old job?" If you buy a new house, "What was wrong with the old house?" If you buy a new car, "What was wrong with the old car?" Or they may say instead, "Well, it's about time you changed jobs," or, "You mean you finally gave up on that old junker and bought a new car?" Because of this kind of programming, people have the feeling that if they change they are admitting to the whole world that what they were doing was wrong or that the change may be wrong.

It is because of this kind of programming with right and wrong that we hang onto our problems. We don't want to let go of them. You've all experienced this. I'm sure you've had a friend who came to you with a problem and from your perspective you could see the perfect answer for your friend. So you told them that answer. Did they accept it? No, in fact if you continue pushing the perfect answer on them, what will they do? They will find a new friend; someone who doesn't have the answer. So it becomes a paradox, doesn't it? We want to solve our problems and yet we are reluctant to exchange them for answers. Now if we are going to continue in this rut, hanging onto our problems so we won't be wrong, then how might we solve this paradox? How might we keep problems and find answers at the same time?

The answer is very simple. Simply create new problems. As soon as you create a new problem you are willing to let go of an old problem. If you would allow me to, I could eliminate every problem in your life except one. If you were to put your arm across a chopping block, and let me chop off your hand, as you watched your lifeless hand lay there, I guarantee you, you wouldn't have another problem in the world. I would have just given you a new problem that's bigger and better than all the rest of your problems put together and so you would be willing to let go of all those other problems and focus on your new problem. This is why many people who have had a severe traumatic experience, such as a heart attack or a severe accident have later said it was a blessing in disguise, it was the greatest thing that ever happened to them and because of it, they completely changed their lives for the better. This happened because their new problem was so big that it caused them to stop thinking of all their other problems and hang-ups. And by the time they solved the new one, they forgot all the old ones.

Because of our right and wrong programming we spend more time on problems than we do on answers, and because of this, problems become more important than answers. Who are the highest paid people in the world? Problem solvers!? No. Who are the highest paid people in a corporation? The president and the vice president. And who create all the problems in a corporation? The president and the vice president-- and the employees solve them. It is the problem creators who are the highest paid. It's only natural if you create the problem of building a ten-story building, you are naturally going to receive greater pay than for creating the problem of building a one-story building. The bigger the problems you can create in life for people to solve, the more money you are going to earn because everybody is programmed that you must have problems to find answers. And yet, at the same time, people are very reluctant to give up the problem in exchange for an answer.

Can you understand why you are so reluctant to exchange your problems for answers? It's because of your fear of being wrong creating your need to be right. Understand, a problem cannot make you wrong. Have you ever had the wrong problem in your life? No, but how many times in your life have you been told you had the wrong answer? You see, as long as you are working with the problem, you can't be wrong. No one will disagree with you. But as soon as you come up with an answer there always seem to be several people around who disagree. People seldom ever judge problems but we really get into judging answers. If someone says."I've got a problem," we listen eagerly and usually with agreement. If someone says,"I've got an answer," we listen skeptically and many times with disagreement. So as long as you remain undecided, no one will say you are wrong. But the moment you make a decision you are taking a chance on being wrong.

This is demonstrated many times by students taking an examination. Many times you will see a student waste a third of the period before he puts down the answer to the first question. Once he has answered the first question, then he will very rapidly go on through the test and answer the rest of the questions. The reason he puts off answering the first question is because he knows he cannot be wrong until he puts down the first answer. Once he has written down the first answer, he has taken a chance on being wrong and so he might as well go ahead and take the chance of answering the rest of the questions wrong.

Being wrong seems to be about the worst thing that can happen to a person. You can cuss your friends out, call them names, tell them they're ugly, almost anything, and still get along with them. But tell them they are wrong about one or two little things and immediately you've got an argument or you lose a friend. It seems as though the worst thing in the world is being wrong, but if you go through life always doing the right thing, you're going through life how? You're going through life doing what everyone else agrees that you should do.

We are living in a day and age, though, when we can begin to base our decisions on the answers and results in life we desire rather than on this tremendous need to be right and the fear of being wrong. We see this already happening with the youth today. The teenager comes in and says to his parents, "I'm dropping out of school," and mom and dad say, "You can't do that! Its wrong." What's the youth's answer? "What's wrong with it?" Youth today are experiencing a great deal of freedom from the judgment of right and wrong. If the older generation could only understand this, they would give the youth of today some beautiful guidance in the decisions they face.

When the youth comes in and announces he's going to drop out of school, don't tell him it's wrong. Tell him its O.K. After all, some of the greatest leaders in the world never completed school. The role of the parent is to help the youth become aware of the probable results of dropping out of school, as well as the probable results of completing his schooling. Let the child be aware that if he drops out of school he will probably have greater problems in getting work and when he does get work it will probably be at a lower salary. This will probably cause problems in supporting his family. He may never be able to buy a new home or the new cars and clothes that he desires. He will probably never be able to travel as much as he desires. And he may go through life wishing he had completed school. Those are some of the probable results of dropping out of school. But that's O.K. because all the people who have dropped out of school are O.K. people too. If he continues through school, the probabilities are that it will be easier for him to find work and he will receive a higher salary for the work that he does. Therefore, he'll be able to travel more, have better vacations, buy new cars, new homes, and other things he desires, and that's O.K. too.

You see, your job is to point out the probable results

of either decision, and then the child can base his decision on those results that will best express his inner perfection. If a youth drops out of school and the parent knows it is wrong to drop out, what is the youth admitting if he goes back to school? He's admitting to his parents he was wrong. But if it's O.K. to drop out, if it's just that he may not have the results he wants in life, then he can later go back to school and not be wrong. Most parents will not admit to being wrong about anything to their children and yet in guiding their children they constantly make the children admit they're wrong and then they wonder why there is a generation gap, why they can't communicate with their children.

If you go through life hanging onto right and wrong as a guideline to perfection, this means you will always be trying to find the right answer, the one that most people agree with. Isn't it true? Haven't you gone through life always trying to do the right thing, say the right thing, be the right thing, always trying to find the right answers? Haven't you realized by now that the right answer does not always give you the best results? How many times in life have you said to yourself, "How did I ever get into this mess?" You got yourself into that mess because you accepted the right answers, the answers that other people agreed were right for you. How many times have you found yourself experiencing something like a really bad hangover. If you would reflect back on the reason, you would find that many times it happened because you did the right thing. Someone else kept telling you it was right to have another drink and you accepted the right answer. This is O.K. if you want the result of a hangover but understand it came from being right.

How many times have we seen a boy and a girl going together and mother and father agree that they are right for each other and should get married. All of their friends agree they are a perfect match and should get married, and so they accept the right answer and get married. Three years later they are divorced. It may have been the right answer, but was it the kind of result they wanted in their lives?

Many times the answer which gives us the best results may have nothing to do with the problem itself. An example might be the man who has let his job or business run his whole life to the exclusion of all outside interests. For fifteen or twenty years he has lived it and breathed it, day in and day out. At about forty years of age, he has a heart attack. He goes to the hospital and the doctors tell him, "You've got to slow down. You must get yourself some outside interests and leave the office a little more. You've got to get out and relax and enjoy life for a change." And so the man takes the doctor's advice. He starts fishing and hunting, hiking, and camping, and as he gets involved in these activities he says, "Wow! This is living. For the first time in my life I'm really enjoying life." He's found an answer. Now did the problem of the heart attack have anything to do with that answer? No, that answer had existed all of his life. Twenty years ago he could have started fishing, hunting, camping, and enjoying life, and he probably would have never had the heart attack.

From this example you can begin to really understand what causes problems. What caused the problem of the heart attack? It's simple. The answer caused the problem. **Answers cause problems,** and it's only when you ignore the answer that you are aware of a problem. The answer always comes first. You will never be aware of a problem except that the answer existed before the problem. Two plus two is a problem, isn't it? But that could not be a problem except that there is already the answer, four. If the answer, four, did not already exist, two plus two simply could not be a problem. In youth we had the perspective that answers created problems. When the teacher put a big problem on the chalkboard, we didn't panic. Why? Because we knew there was already an answer. How would you have felt if your teacher put a problem on the chalkboard and said, "Nobody in the world knows the answer to this problem. Now figure it out." Understand that it is answers that cause problems, and the only time we have a problem is when we do not see the answer.

Most often we do not see the answers simply because we are afraid of being wrong. If you have a fear of being wrong you are constantly looking for the wrong thing so that you can avoid it. The wrong thing is called a "problem." We usually find what we are looking for as we go through life. If you are constantly looking for a problem so that you can avoid it, then you always find the problem. If you let go of the fear of being wrong, your mind will stop seeking the wrong thing so that you can avoid it and will see the answers instead of the problems.

Let me give you an example. We have two skiers standing at the top of the ski hill. Between them and the bottom of the hill are about a hundred moguls, the large bumps in the snow which are the fear of many skiers. One skier stands at the top of the hill and looks down and sees one hundred gigantic problems. There are one hundred moguls that somehow he's got to get around or over or under or through to get to the bottom of the hill. So he stands at the top of the hill and looks at his first problem, the first mogul, and figures out an answer. He decides he can turn around the left edge. And then he looks at his next problem, the next mogul, and he figures out an answer for it. He might be able to turn right on top of it. The third mogul is a little too far away, and he can't quite figure out the answer. As he starts down the hill, he makes it around and over the first and second moguls because he has already figured out the answers. When he comes to the third mogul, he figures out the answer just in time. But by the time he gets to the fourth mogul, he's too late. He cannot see the answer in time and what happens? He does the wrong thing, he falls down. Then he stands up on top of that mogul and figures out answers to his next two or three problems. Then he starts again, but by the fourth or fifth mogul, he's too late finding his answer and he falls down again. Because this skier sees one hundred problems between himself and the bottom of the hill, he must find one hundred answers to get to the bottom.

Understand the reason he saw the problems is because he was afraid of doing the wrong thing. The wrong thing on a ski hill is falling down. Since he was worried about falling down, his mind was constantly looking for all the ways and all the places that he might fall down so that he could avoid them.

The second skier stands at the top of the same hill with the same one hundred moguls, and he looks down and sees one hundred beautiful answers. There are one hundred moguls to help him turn to get down the hill, and he simply goes down the hill turning back and forth from one answer to the next. Now which skier do you suppose experiences less effort, less frustration, getting to the bottom of the hill? Of course, it's the one that's flowing with the universe.

You have probably seen two individuals doing exactly the same job. One individual just barely gets started and he says, "Wait a minute now, I have a problem." So he stops and figures out the answer to the problems and starts again. After he has done a little more, again he says, "Wait a minute, I have another problem." And again he stops and figures the answer. And so he goes through the job seeing problems and stopping to figure out the answers. The other individual, doing exactly the same job, simply starts in doing the job and keeps doing it until he finishes. He just sees the answers. The answers had to be there to begin with or the first individual could never have figured them out. Can you understand that if he had seen the answers first he would have never seen the problems, would he? The reason he saw the problems is because he was afraid of doing the wrong thing. Consequently, he kept looking for the wrong thing so that he could avoid it. Each time he saw a wrong way of doing the job he called it a problem and he had to stop and figure out a way to avoid it. The second individual doing the job had no fear of doing the wrong thing. Therefore, he didn't become aware of any wrong things to avoid.

If you were to spend time with these two individuals you would see two very different personalities. The first individual who saw all of the problems would be very judgmental and critical. He goes through life constantly criticizing things and people. As I said before, you always get back more criticism than you put out. It's a beautiful example of the ten-fold return. Since he is receiving more criticism than he's giving, he naturally develops a fear of being criticized so his mind always looks for things he might be criticized for so he can avoid them. Every time he sees something he might be criticized for, he calls it a problem and he has to figure out the answer to avoid being wrong.

The second individual's personality would be non-judgmental, non-critical. Therefore, he would have no fear of being criticized or judged. Since he has no fear of being wrong his mind does not seek wrong things to avoid and he sees the answers instead. Remember, the answer always has to be there or you cannot have a problem.

It is answers that create problems, but unfortunately all of our lives we have been taught exactly the opposite. We have been taught to look for the problem and through the problem find the answer. As you were going through school, did the teacher ever put the answer up on the chalkboard and then tell you to figure out all of the problems that could be caused by that answer? No, she always put the problem up first and then asked you to figure out the answer from the problem.

I am simply saying that if you go through life looking for problems, you have a tendency to find problems. If you go through life looking for answers, the tendency is to find answers. If you are strongly programmed with right/wrong judgment, this causes your mind to seek out wrong things (called problems) so that you can avoid them. If you will let go of right and wrong in terms of judgment, your mind will naturally see more answers instead of problems.

IT'S O.K.

Now, if you want to start seeing answers instead of problems, let me share with you the GREATEST PROBLEM SOLVING CONCEPT IN THE UNIVERSE. To use this problem solving concept all you need to do is simply understand that all problems are O.K. Every problem you have is O.K. The problem, itself, is O.K.; and it's O.K. for you to be experiencing the problem. It's O.K. if you are unhappily married. It's O.K. if you are overweight. It's O.K. if you can't pay your bills. If you want to solve your problems, you must first realize your problems are O.K.

The reason problems must be O.K. is because your brain operates under the law, "as you believe so shall it be done." Your brain is a computer-like guidance mechanism and it guides you according to the beliefs you have programmed it with. However, there are different degrees of belief. What are some of the things you believe in? You might answer God, gravity, myself, night and day. These are things we might all believe in, but there are things we believe in stronger than any of these. The simple truth is that the things we believe in stronger than anything else

are the things that we fear. I will guarantee you, if you
are walking down a narrow path through the woods
and you come face to face with a grizzly bear, you are
going to believe in that grizzly bear stronger than you
ever believed in God or gravity or yourself or
anything else. If you believed in God that strongly,
you would be getting answers to all your prayers, but
you've probably never prayed with that much energy
and emotion. You see, fear is the same thing as belief
except that you put more energy and emotion into
something you fear and so it becomes a stronger
belief.

You believe in God. You believe in yourself. You
believe in gravity. That is believing. Then there is
really believing, and really believing is worrying
about something. Worrying about being overweight
or being depressed is simply really believing in being
fat or being unhappy. And then there is really, really
believing. And the things in life you really, really
believe in are the things in life you fear. If you have a
fear of being in debt or a fear of the darkness, you
simply really, really believe in being broke or you
really, really believe in the boogieman. Realize that
you use the same faculties of your brain-mind
functioning to believe in God as you use to fear the
dentist, except that when your believing reaches the
degree of fear, you are putting more energy and more
emotion into it so it becomes a stronger belief.

If you can grasp the fact that worry and fear are the
strongest forms of believing, and as you believe so
shall it be done unto you, then you will understand
how allowing your problems to be O.K. will solve 90%
of your problems in life without even directing any

attention to the problem. The simplicity that makes this work is this simple. Have you ever worried about something or feared something if you knew it was O.K. No! If something is O.K., you do not worry about it or fear it. I wish I could explain this to you in some very intricate, difficult, complicated terms. Then you might say, "Oh, it's simple; I understand it." Well, I apologize, I cannot complicate it. This concept is so simple I cannot make it difficult for you. So circle with it like the jet over the car until you grasp the simplicity of it.

The reason you have failed to reach many of your goals in life is because you have not been aware that worry and fear are the strongest forms of belief. It doesn't do you any good to go on a diet and starve yourself three meals a day believing you are going to lose weight and then spend the rest of the day worrying about gaining weight, because what you are doing is really believing in gaining weight. There is an ancient message, "That which I feared the most came upon me." What the message is really saying is, that which I really, really believed in happened to me.

Worry and fear are mostly subconcious functions. If you are deeply in debt and cannot pay your bills, you do not have to write yourself little notes to remind yourself to worry about your bills. You automatically worry about them whether you consciously remind yourself or not.

If you almost have an auto accident, you don't consciously say to yourself, "I've been frightened and so now I'll experience fear." You automatically experience the fear without consciously thinking about it.

If you are constantly worrying about or fearing something, the greater energy and emotion from the worry and the fear create a predominant brain cell pattern of what you are fearing or worrying about. Your predominant brain cell patterns are your habits or your comfort zones. Fear and worry simply develop a habit of being or doing or having what you fear or what you worry about.

If you consciously desire and strive to lose weight and yet at the same time you are constantly worrying about gaining weight, the greater energy of worry is making a predominant brain cell pattern for gaining weight. That predominant pattern is then controlled by the subconscious mind as an attitude or habit for gaining weight. So ultimately you have the conscious mind saying, "I must lose weight," and the subconscious mind saying, "I must gain weight," and which usually wins? Yes, the subconscious mind.

You have probably experienced the frustration, the depression, the tension of that battle going on between your conscious desires and your subconscious habits. How many times have you said to yourself, "I don't know why I keep doing this. I really don't want to but I can't seem to stop?" Haven't you found yourself consciously praying to stop something and at the same time worrying to keep it going--praying to get out of debt and worrying to stay in debt, praying to lose weight and worrying to gain weight.

If you will allow your problems to be O.K. just the way they are, then your subconscious mind will stop worrying about them or stop fearing them. This allows your subconscious mind to stop really, really believing in your problems. Then the conscious desire or answer has a chance to become a reality. In other words, by eliminating worry and fear you allow your mind to see answers instead of problems.

You have probably experienced this sometime during your education. Can you recall taking a test that you were not prepared for and yet at the same time you were not worried about failing it? For some reason it just didn't seem that important and when you received your grade, to your surprise, you got an exceptionally high score. This happened because you were not worrying about the problems and you allowed your mind to see the answers. Can you recall taking another test which you had spent hours studying for, but you were still worrying about failing and, sure enough, you did? Even after all your preparation you failed. This happened because your worry created a subconscious belief in failing the test.

Your brain is designed in a computer-like manner to seek answers, but through worry and fear you have taught it to see the problems instead. If all of your attention is focused on the problem, you will not see the answer. If all of your brain-mind-body energy is focused on depression, then it is impossible to see happiness. **Worry simply develops a habit of having or doing or being what you are worrying about.**

Remember I said that if you allow all of your problems to be O.K., this will solve 90% of your problems in life without even being concerned with the problem. The other 10% you must objectively do something about as well as know that they are O.K. If you go out to get in your car and it has a flat tire, you can sit down beside your car and say, "It's O.K., O.K.,

O.K.," as long as you want and twenty-four hours later the tire will still be flat. This is one of the problems in life that fall in that 10% that you must objectively do something to solve, and yet if it's O.K. for you to have a flat tire, you have solved 90% of the problem of a flat tire. If you will allow the 10% of your problems that you have to physically, objectively solve to be O.K., it will solve 90% of each one of them.

I'm sure you've all seen a person with a flat tire who knows flat tires are not O.K. When do they usually have their flats? Sure. When they are in a last-minute rush to get somewhere, or when it's raining, or on an overpass on the freeway. Then, cussing and swearing, they get out of the car and nearly break their toe kicking the flat tire. Then they get the key stuck in the trunk. When they finally get the jack out they drop it on their toe. After they get the car jacked up, it slides off the jack. Finally, an hour later, all messed up and dirty, angry at the whole world, they get the tire changed and are on their way. Isn't this the way it usually happens with the person who hates to have flat tires?

You have also seen the person have a flat tire who knows it is O.K. to have flat tires and, whistling or singing, he gets out of the car, opens the trunk, takes out the jack and the spare, jacks up the car, takes off the flat, puts on the spare, puts the flat tire and jack back in the trunk, and ten minutes later, still at peace with the whole world, he is on his way. That is the simplicity of realizing your problems are O.K.

When you start using this concept, start with yourself, because if you are not O.K., then nothing else in the world is O.K. Have you noticed that when you are not O.K., then nothing is O.K. When you are filled with happiness, when you are O.K., the whole universe and everything in it is O.K. **So start with yourself being O.K.**

If you have a problem seeing yourself being O.K. just the way you are, with all of your hang-ups, then stop and think of all the other people you know who are O.K. just the way they are, with all of their hang-ups. Don't you have some really wonderful friends who are overweight? And overweight just like they are, they are O.K. Churchill was overweight, but wasn't he a beautiful person. If Churchill and all the overweight people you know can be O.K. being overweight, then so can you. Do you have some really wonderful freinds who have no money and are deeply in debt and yet they are still O.K.? If these people can be broke and O.K., so can you. Do you know some really wonderful people who are depressed but yet they are O.K.? If they can be depressed and be O.K., then so can you. If you realize that all of these people are O.K. just the way they are, even with all of their hang-ups, then it is easier for you to be O.K., just the way you are.

In fact, when we really stop and think about it, throughout the ages, even the most loved and respected people in the world die. If even the greatest people who live still die, then it must be O.K. for us to die. If you fear death, you are really, really believing in your death and that may certainly cause it to happen sooner.

So as you start using this O.K. concept, start by letting yourself be O.K., but start with little things. I mean, don't take chances on starting with something

big like, it's O.K. to quit your job or tell your boss off.
Or, it's O.K. to have cancer or a heart attack or to be
an alcoholic. Just start with the little things, like it's
O.K. to bite your fingernails. It's O.K. if you have
freckles. It's O.K. if you have a big nose. It's O.K. if
someone dislikes you. Just keep telling yourself these
things are O.K. Suddenly one day to your amazement
you will find they really are O.K. You will find you no
longer have the need to bite your fingernails or you
may be like the starlet who became a world famous
star because she knew her freckles were O.K., and so
the whole world learned to love them. You may find
you have a nose like Jimmy Durante, which was loved
and respected by the entire world. If it's O.K. if
someone dislikes you, you may develop some of the
attributes of President Lincoln. Edwin Stanton,
whom Lincoln appointed Secretary of War, despised
Lincoln and publicly denounced him at every
opportunity. Still, to Lincoln, Stanton was O.K. No
wonder Stanton stood sobbing at Lincoln's bedside
after the assassination and publicly declared, "There
lies the greatest ruler of men the world has ever
seen."

As you begin to allow your little problems in life to be
O.K. and you see them dissolve and dissipate, you will
understand how you may use the O.K. concept to
help you solve any problems in life, big or small. You
will understand it really is O.K. to be disappointed or
depressed, to be discouraged or unhappy. It really is
O.K. if you are ugly or too fat or too skinny. It's O.K.
to be unhappily married or in debt. It's O.K. to be ill or
even to be an alcoholic. As you allow your problems
to be O.K., you will understand that this causes the

subconscious mind to stop worrying about or fearing the problem and allows the conscious mind to focus upon the answer. Once you realize you are O.K. just the way you are, you will have found a beautiful freedom to change and become anything you desire. This is simply because your subconscious mind will stop believing in your hang-ups.

Please circle with this concept until you understand that allowing the problem to be O.K. is simply a way of releasing the problem. It does not mean that allowing the problem to be O.K. is agreeing to live with the problem the rest of your life. If you have acrophobia, a fear of heights, letting it be O.K. simply releases the subconscious fear. This then helps you experience your conscious desire to enjoy high places. If someone dislikes you, your letting it be O.K. stops your subconscious belief in his dislike and when that happens you will find that you can like him and he can like you.

When you worry, you create a predominant brain cell pattern of the problem. When you say it's O.K. you are creating a new pattern that releases the worry and thereby releases the problem. You may ask, "Well, how long does it take?" That depends on how predominant the brain cell pattern created by the worry is. Maybe part of the answer is in the verse, "Forgive your enemies until seventy times seven." Each time you say it's O.K. you will realize it has a beneficial effect. If you keep applying the concept and allow all problems to be O.K., eventually you will create a new predominant brain cell pattern that simply says, "problems are O.K."

After you have experienced the ah-hah that you

really are O.K. just the way you are, then you may experience another ah-hah, that every other person in the world is O.K. too, just the way they are. Even though it may seem like an impossiblity at the moment, if you keep applying this O.K. concept, one day you will realize that even your husband or wife, your parents or your children, your boss and even your enemies are O.K., just the way they are. In understanding this you will have developed a powerful tool in helping other people overcome their problems.

If your child is smoking and you know it's not O.K. to smoke, what is your child admitting if he stops smoking? That's correct, your child is admitting he was wrong. But, if it's O.K. to smoke and it's simply that the results of smoking through a lifetime are usually not desirable, then the child can quit smoking without being wrong.

It's this concept that has given me so much success in communicating with youth about their problems. So many times parents will drag their child in, sure that I am going to tell the child how wrong he is for smoking or drinking or taking dope or whatever it may be. As soon as the parents leave the room, my communication with the youth is that his problem is O.K. I mean, it really is O.K. to take dope. It's even O.K. to shoot heroin. The result of shooting heroin is that you will probably die within four years because that is the average lifetime of a mainliner. That's O.K. too because we've all got to die sooner or later and if they choose to do it in that manner and that soon, that's O.K. too. I also point out to the youth the probable results of letting go of dope which is probably a longer, healthier, happier life.

I really communicate with youth that they are O.K. with problems or without them. It's only that the results are going to be different one way or the other. This allows youth to let go of problems without being wrong.

This O.K. concept is not new to you. You have already used this concept to solve some of your biggest problems in life. When you faced a problem and you knew there was nothing you could do about it, there was nothing you could do to change the situation, many times you have said, "Well, there is nothing I can do about it, so I guess it's O.K." And what happened? Most often this caused you to stop worrying about the problem and the problem dissolved and disappeared.

If you will really mull this over in your mind and mentally digest it, then one day you will experience the ah-hah that at this moment the whole world is O.K., just the way it is. At this moment the whole universe is O.K. just like it is. Circle with me and you will begin to see the perfection of the universe and understand more of the now moment. You see, in the now moment which is already past, circle with me now, in the now instant which is already gone, which is already past, in that instant which is now history, there was nothing more you could do to change yourself, was there? Most people agree, if there is absolutely nothing you can do to change something, then it is O.K. just the way it is. So for that instant you had to be O.K. just like you were.

Circle with me again. In the now instant, which is past, which is gone forever, in that instant there was nothing more you could do to change anybody else. So in that instant everyone else was O.K. just the way they were. Circle with me again. In the now instant, which is past, which is gone forever, in that instant there was nothing more you could do to change the world, was there? So in that instant the whole world was O.K. just as it was. In the now moment, which has already past, in that instant which is now history, there was nothing more you could do to change the universe, was there? So in that instant the universe was O.K. just the way it was.

Now you might ask, "If the whole world is O.K. and every person is O.K. and all problems are O.K., just the way they are, then why change? Why put out any effort? Why do anything at all?" There is no reason to do anything, there is no reason to change, unless you want to experience something different than you are experiencing now. If you are experiencing an unhappy marriage and instead you would like to experience a happy marriage, then of course, you must change. If you want that change to take place without frustration and without problems, if you want that change to take place by flowing with the universe, then you must first realize that it is O.K. to be experiencing an unhappy marriage now. This will allow your subconscious mind and those people around you the freedom to begin experiencing a happy marriage.

PLEASE UNDERSTAND, ALLOWING EVERYTHING TO BE O.K. DOES NOT STOP CHANGE AND PROGRESS, INSTEAD IT ALLOWS PERFECT CHANGE AND PROGRESS TO TAKE PLACE WITHOUT PROBLEMS. If the problem is not O.K. this forces you to keep the problem in your mind and you take the problem into the future. If the problem is O.K., this allows your mind to release the problem and leave it in the past so that you can see the answer in the future. If you are aware of a problem, that indicates a conscious desire to solve it. Allowing a problem to be O.K. eliminates the worry and frustration which helps your conscious mind see answers instead of magnifying the problem.

You may still misunderstand this whole concept and say, "But what if someone takes unfair advantage of me--is that O.K.?" Sure, it's O.K. if someone takes unfair advantage of you. If you had allowed it to be O.K. before it happened, it probably would never have happened. Haven't you noticed that the people who are always worried (really believing) that someone is going to take advantage of them are the ones who are usually taken advantage of? Even more important is understanding you are O.K. and so it's O.K. for you to do something about it. It's O.K. for you to do something to make them stop taking advantage of you. You see, the whole universe is O.K. When you only use the concept halfway, you only get half the results. When you say it's O.K. for someone to take unfair advantage of you, but it's not O.K. for you to do something about it you are only using it halfway. When you say it is not O.K. for someone to take unfair advantage of me but it is O.K. for me to do something about it, you are only using the concept halfway. It's all O.K. Allowing it to be O.K. for people to take advantage of you does not guarantee that no one will. However, it does stop you from believing that everyone is going to take advantage of you and, consequently, fewer people do. **Letting it be O.K. to fail does not guarantee success but it will stop you from believing in failure which will certainly make your success a lot easier.**

If your problems are not O.K., then through your worry or fear or guilt or anger or resentment or depression your subconscious mind keeps the problems with you day after day. If you allow the problem to be O.K. then the subconscious mind releases it and leaves the problem behind. When you leave the problem behind it naturally causes things to start changing and soon you have your answer.

As you begin using the O.K. concept I really encourage you to start with small problems. Start with the little things that frustrate or worry you. As you see these small problems dissolve and disappear you will understand how you can use this concept on larger problems. You will understand how you can apply it to your fears and phobias. You will understand how you can even apply it to state, country, and world problems. If you start using the concept with big problems in the beginning, many times the impossibility seems so great you lose your perspective before you even get started.

Circle with this O.K. concept until you grasp it, because it is what allows you to see answers instead of problems. It allows you to discipline your children without being angry. It allows you to accomplish a whole day's work and yet not feel worked. It will allow you to rush in life and not be rushed. Haven't you experienced the tension and frustration of rushing down the highway at 65 miles per hour trying to get some place on time, really feeling rushed, and then again some Sunday, driving along pleasantly relaxed at the same 65 miles per hour, not feeling rushed at all? What's the difference? You were going 65 miles per hour both times. The difference is that on the Sunday drive it was O.K. if you didn't drive 65 miles per hour and on the other trip it was not O.K. if you didn't drive 65 miles per hour.

The most important reason for applying the O.K. concept is to eliminate fear, worry, guilt, and judgment. Fear, worry, guilt, and judging are four of the most destructive forces there are. If you allow yourself and your problems to be O.K. and other people and their problems to be O.K., you eliminate the need of worry, fear, guilt, and judgment from your life.

The reason there is so much power in realizing that yourself and your problems and everyone else and the whole world is O.K. is because letting it be O.K. is a lot closer to love than what you have been calling love. How many times have you said to your husband or wife or parents or children or boy friend or girl friend, "I love you anyway."" What you are really saying is that you are not O.K., but I love you anyway. And, friends, that is not love. Instead, when you can say to your friends, to your family, to your enemies, "You are O.K. just the way you are," that is love.

It has been said that **love** is the strongest force in the universe, that **love** overcometh all things. If this is true, then love should certainly overcome our problems. If the power of love will solve our problems, then maybe we ought to analyze what love really is. Love is what? What are some one-word definitions for love? Love is happiness. Love is caring.

Love is sharing. Love is empathy. Love is friendship, charity, kindness, believing in someone. These are all beautiful definitions of love, and we can go on and on with hundreds more like them.

Yet isn't it amazing and possibly amusing that if we were to pick one hundred people at random and ask them to tell us the story of their love lives from day one until now, do you suppose we would get the story of happiness and caring and sharing and kindness? Probably not. From nearly every one of them we would get a long tale of woe and misery, of heartaches and heartbreaks. Now something is out of balance. Either we don't know the correct definition of love, or we don't know how to experience it.

Maybe we can arrive at a more correct definition of love through a different analysis. We might ask, what is the Creator? God is what? What are some one-word definitions for God? Nearly any place we ask this question, within the first answer or two, someone always answers God is love. Certainly of all the things that the Creator is, one thing we might agree upon is that "God is love." So maybe then we could ask ourselves what does the Creator give us as love? Someone answers life. So we ask one hundred people picked at random to tell the story of their lives. Now do you suppose we would get any kind of story that matches our definition of love--a story of happiness, caring, sharing, kindness, friendship. No. Again, the majority of the stories would be of heartaches and heartbreaks. So it is true our Creator gives us life, but that must not be what He gives us as love.

Someone else may say freedom. And so we ask a

hundred people to tell us the story of all the freedom they've experienced in their lives and again their stories don't come anywhere near matching our definition of love. Someone may say, He gives us forgiveness as love. And so we ask a hundred people to tell about all the forgiveness they've received in their lives. And that story only takes each of them a few seconds to tell. If forgiveness is what they are receiving as love, they certainly haven't received very much of it.

We could go on and on and probably take hours before we arrived at a correct answer, because it is the simplicity of love that eludes us. What the Creator gives you as love is He simply grants you the being, to be that which you are, and not be that which you are not. God grants you the being to be whatever you are, and not be whatever you are not and that is love. That is the one thing we can define as love that will result in all of the other things we have been calling love-- happiness, the caring, the sharing, the kindness, the hugs, and the kisses. Those are the results of love, the results of granting being.

It is very important that the Creator grants us the being to not be that which we are not. Because, you see the possibilities of all that we could be during this life extend almost into infinity. We could be a truck driver or a dentist, a farmer, lawyer, secretary, banker, maid, teacher, merchant, minister, sailor, soldier. And in the one hundred years or less that we have to be here, we only have time to be a few of these. And the list still goes on. We could be a doctor, a housewife, a typist, a baker, a bum, rich, poor, fat, skinny, happy, depressed, and on and on. In the short lifetime of the human being we only have time to be just a few of the things, compared to the list of possible things that we could be. So it is very fortunate that the Creator doesn't say, "You are wrong. You must stop being a nurse. You have to be a school teacher." If you want to be a nurse, the Creator simply grants you the being to be a nurse. And if you're not being a school teacher, the Creator grants you the being not to be a school teacher. The Creator does not reach out and slap your hands and say, "You must stop being sad, you have to be happy." You see, if you do not want to be happy, the Creator grants you the being to not be happy. The Creator doesn't reach out and slap your hands and say, "You must stop being a failure." If you want to be a failure, God grants you the being to be a failure and grants you the being to not be successful.

Any two human beings, husband and wife, parent and child, employer and employee, business partners, friends, neighbors, enemies, any two people in any situation in life, who will grant each other being, to be anything they are and not be anything they are not, will experience all the caring, sharing, kindness, and other things that we originally called love when we tried to define it.

Probably the greatest example of granting being is in the immortal message, "Become as a little child." A mind-opening example can be demonstrated from the love given to mother and father from a three-or four-year-old child in drastic comparison to the granting of being between the husband and wife. Mother and father can come home from their party and pass out on the living room floor, dead drunk, and the little three-or four-year-old child will still love them. To him they are still O.K. just the way they are. He grants them the being to be whatever they are and not be whatever they are not. How much being would a husband grant his wife if she staggered in from her party and passed out on the living room floor? The little child will express love even when mother and father are fighting and quarreling. He will grant them the being to be what they are and what they are not. How much being do parents grant their children when the children are quarreling? The little child will grant being to mother or father to scold him or spank him. He will still express love to his mother when the house is dirty, the dishes aren't washed, and supper's not ready. He grants her the being to be what she is and not be what she is not. The little child will express love to his father when there is no money to buy food, there is no money for toys and the house is cold. He grants him the being to be what he is and what he is not. The little child will grant his parents being to be happy or depressed, to be angry or kind, to be gentle or rough, to succeed or fail, to live in poverty or abundance, to be healthy or ill, to complain or to be cheerful, to be fat or skinny, to be beautiful or to be ugly, no matter what mother and father are, no matter what they do, no matter what they have, to the little child they are O.K., just the way they are. No wonder "One must become as a little child to enter the kingdom of heaven."

Understand now why the O.K. concept is the most powerful problem solving concept in the universe. When you know that a problem or yourself or another person is O.K. just the way they are, you are expressing love, and love truly is the greatest power in the universe. Love, truly, overcometh all things. **"It's O.K.", is the expressing of love.**

There is a fascinating, mind-expanding aspect about love in that you can only give love, you cannot keep it. You can give love to another person but they cannot keep your love. I grant you being, I give you love; accept or reject these concepts, like them or dislike them, believe them or disbelieve them, use them or don't use them, it's O.K. I grant you that being. I give you that expression of love, but I haven't really given you anything that you can keep. That is why love is the strongest force in the universe. Whenever love is expressed, nothing can stop it. It keeps spreading throughout the universe because it cannot be possessed.

You may say, but when people love me and I have their love it makes me feel good. But you do not have their love because having indicates possession. If you really become aware, you will find that it's not having love that makes you feel good, but rather it's returning it or passing it on. This is part of the ancient message, "It is more blessed to give than it is to receive." It is more blessed to give love, to grant being, than it is to receive it, because you can't keep it anyway.

The reason it is more blessed to give love than to receive it is because you are giving of your real true self. If you take a human being and take away the human part, all you have left is the being and that part of you is love. You are like a container of honey. The outside of the container may be totally camouflaged, it may be too big or too little, it may be ugly or dirty, and yet within the container the honey still remains pure and sweet. This same thing is true of you no matter how much fear, hate, sorrow, misery, belief or disbelief, fat, gray hair, or wrinkles you have covered yourself up with. The real you within, your inner-self, still remains beautiful and perfect. If you grasp this, then you may grasp part of the message that says,"The truth shall set you free." The truth is that the real you, your inner-self is love. And when you give of yourself you may truly overcome all things. If you will project your love into a problem, in other words, let the problem be O.K. just the way it is, you will become free of the problem.

Some of the most important problems to grant being to are your fears, your worries, and your complexes. If you have a fear of being alone at night or being in darkness, grant it being, keep telling yourself it's O.K. to be alone in darkness and it's also O.K. to fear the darkness. This allows your subconscious mind to let go of the fear, and your conscious mind is then free from the fear of darkness. Understand that the real you, your inner-self, cannot be harmed in any way in darkness. Therefore, the real you, the part of you that is love, cannot fear darkness.

If you have a fear of death, keep telling yourself death is O.K., and it's O.K. to fear death. This, again, allows your subconscious mind freedom from the fear of death. Understand that the real you, your inner-self, cannot fear death, because your inner-self cannot die. If you have an inferiority complex and you are O.K. just like you are, very soon you will find this expression of love will dissipate the complex and you will have found your freedom from the inferiority complex.

Probably the most rewarding demonstration of granting being is in your relationships with other people. If you do not get along with your boss, grant him being, allow him to be O.K. just the way he is with all of his hang-ups. Very soon you'll realize you like your boss and even more amazing you will find your boss likes you. The reason for this is because, more so than anything else, love returns itself. When you grant your boss being, he cannot keep that love, he must pass it on. And like most people he will usually give it back to its source. When you give love to your boss, since he cannot keep it, he will express that same love back to you immediately. Use it, it really works.

As an example of love returning itself, when I repeat the Alpha Awareness Training course in a city, I always have many former students bring their friends to go through the training. I've asked former students what do you suppose would happen if, after one of the breaks, I walked up to the lectern stark naked? They all agree, their friends would start elbowing them, asking them what's wrong with that man? Is he crazy? And they all agree they would immediately start granting being with statements like, "Wait a minute and he'll explain his reason for being nude." In other words, they would start granting me being, to be nude. And they agree it would be because when they went through the training I granted them being, to accept it or reject it, to stay or to leave, to agree with me or disagree with me, to like me or dislike me. As they went through the training I granted them the being to be whatever they were and not be whatever they were not. And because of that, their natural reaction was to grant me being to be whatever I am and not be whatever I am not. However, please don't be concerned, should you ever attend one of my lectures on Alpha Awareness Training, I promise I will not appear nude.

RESULTS OUTLINE

NAME: _____

DESIRE: _Being rich_

DATE: _____

UNIVERSE FLOWS

WOULD HAVE	WOULDN'T HAVE	WOULD DO	WOULDN'T DO	WOULD BE	WOULDN'T BE
		travel	figure taxes	happy	broke
		study	house work	successful	stingy
		read	scrimp	independent	depressed
		retire	cook	industrious	tense
		sleep late	work at present job	popular	nervous
		write a book		relaxed	inferior
		fish	wear cheap clothes	patient	insecure
		entertain	complain	confident	worried
			eat cheap food	generous	frustrated
				honest	unhappy

COMMENTS: _____

PART II

Now let me share with you a Results Outline which you may use to flow with the universe and be anything in life you truly desire to be. This outline will only be a model. If you want to flow with the universe, without effort and frustration, then I encourage you to make up at least fifteen to twenty similiar outlines for you as an individual. (A completed example is on page 64. This is only an example and is in no way intended for any individual.)

You will begin the outline by deciding something you truly desire to be, such as being happy, successful, relaxed, healthy, or whatever it is you desire to be, and putting that down as the heading. For example, let's use **Being Rich.** Now let's pretend for a moment that you are rich, you are a multimillionaire. What else would you be, being a multimillionaire? You might say happy, so put down happy under the subheading "Would Be." In other words, being rich, you would be happy. As soon as you put down being happy though, several people might disagree, because they think that most rich people are unhappy. One thing you should understand very clearly from this outline is how you have been previously programmed. If you have a strong brain cell impression that rich people are unhappy and you become rich, what else will you be? That's correct, you will also be unhappy. Other things you might add to the list of "Would Be" are successful, independent, industrious, popular, relaxed, patient, confident, generous, honest, etc. However, you must make up this list for you as an individual, as one person may desire to be rich so that he can be lazy.

This list will also help you to become aware of your predominant brain cell patterns relating to being rich. One person may have a predominant brain cell pattern that rich people are generous and another person a predominant brain cell pattern that rich people are stingy. If you bleieve that rich people are generous and you become rich, you will be generous. If you believe that rich people are stingy and you become rich, you will be stingy. There are many people who believe a person must be dishonest to become rich. If you have a brain cell pattern that says rich people are dishonest and you become rich, you will also be dishonest. Many people who have desired to become rich have never become rich because of the subconscious fear of this causing them to be dishonest.

One of the important reasons for making fifteen to twenty outlines of the things you desire to be is that it will make you aware of your opposing brain cell patterns that are blocking you from many of the things you desire. The desire to be rich blocked by the belief that rich people are dishonest. The desire to be happy blocked by the belief that to be happy you must suffer. Your desire to change blocked by the belief that your environment controls you. Your desire to have a happy marriage blocked by the belief that all married couples quarrel. The desire to communicate with your children blocked by the belief that you can't understand them. Nearly all individuals have many beliefs that oppose each other, and this creates frustration. If you have predominant brain cell patterns (habits, attitudes, beliefs, problems) that are blocking things in life that you desire, then I encourage you to purchase the ALPHA AWARENESS TRAINING BOOK as it will teach you how to change the patterns.

When you are making up your individual outlines, I suggest that you put at least ten things under the subheadings "Would Be," "Would Do," "Would Have," and then match them with the same number of things you "Wouldn't Be," "Wouldn't Do," "Wouldn't Have." In the example, page 64, we have listed ten things you "Would Be" and now to balance it out we must list ten things you "Wouldn't Be." Some things that might be suggested are broke, stingy, depressed, tense, nervous, inferior, insecure, worried, frustrated, and unhappy.

Next in the Results Outline of flowing with the universe, are the subheadings of "DO" and "Wouldn't Do." Still pretending that you are a multimillionaire, what ten or more things would you do, being rich? (Before you continue reading, stop and think of ten things you personally would do being rich.) Your list might include such things as travel, study, read, retire, sleep late, write a book, fish, entertain. Understand that when you are making your own individual outline you may put down as many things under each subheading as you desire. However, I suggest you put down at least ten under each subheading. Now let's balance this with things we wouldn't do being rich. What are some of the things now you wouldn't do being rich? The list might include such things as, you wouldn't figure your own taxes, wouldn't do housework, wouldn't scrimp, cook, work at your present job, wear cheap clothes, complain, eat cheap groceries.

To complete the Results Outline of flowing with the universe, let's refer to the subheadings of "Would Have" and "Wouldn't Have." You are rich. You are a multimillionaire. What are some of the things you would have ... a new home, new car, boat, airplane, ranch, mountain cabin, savings account, maid, new furniture, notice how fast the "Have" list comes? Do you understand why? It is because all of your life you have been going against the flow of the universe to become rich. You haven't really thought a lot about being rich. You have mostly thought about having what you would have, after you are rich. In other words, you have been going from **having** into **doing** into **being.** However, that's O.K. because that is the way most of the millionaires in the world have become rich. It's simply that it takes a lot more effort and frustration than flowing with the universe.

Now let's really circle closer so that you might receive another ah-hah. Do you need a million dollars to be happy? No! Do you need even ten cents to be happy? No. Do you need a million dollars to be successful or independent? No. There are people who don't have a dime in their pocket but neither do they owe the world a dime. Do you need a million dollars or even a dime to be industrious or popular or relaxed? No. Nor do you need even a dime to be patient, confident, generous, or honest.

Mull this over and mentally digest it, until you perceive the simplicity of it and receive your ah-hah.

You do not have to have even ten cents to be rich, to be a millionaire. You can be a millionaire at this moment, because all there is to being a millionaire is being the list of things we put under "Would Be."

Would you really want to have a million dollars and all the things on your "Have List"--a new car, your boat, your ranch, your mountain cabin--if you couldn't be happy and generous and successful and popular and relaxed and confident, it wouldn't make any sense, would it? The reason you really wanted to have your car, your new home, your boat, your million dollars is because you thought it would cause you to be all the things on your "Be" list--happy, successful, popular, relaxed, confident. But exactly the opposite is true. It's being all of those things that may cause you to have a million dollars. You may go in either direction. It's simply easier, takes less effort, and you have less frustration if you are flowing with the universe.

Let's take an example of two individuals: one flowing with the universe **being** rich and the other going against the flow of the universe to **become** rich. Let's pretend for a moment that you are president of a large corporation and you are going to hire a top executive in a seventy thousand dollar a year position. Two individuals apply for the position. The first individual has a college education and he has experience in the area you are hiring him for. He is also broke, stingy, depressed, tense, nervous, inferior, insecure. He's frustrated, worried and unhappy. He is being everything on our "Wouldn't Be" list. The second individual does not have a college education nor does he have any experience in the area you are hiring for.

However, he is **being** rich; he's happy; he's independent; successful, industrious, popular, relaxed, patient, confident, generous and honest. This second person is being everything on our "Would Be" list. Now which one of these two individuals would you hire for this seventy thousand dollar a year job? As almost any corporate president would tell you, you would be better off hiring the individual who is already being rich, even though he doesn't have a college education or experience.

It is the individual who starts out being rich who gets the seventy thousand dollar a year job without going through all of the frustration and effort that most people do. One thing rich people usually do is work at high paying jobs which naturally allows them to do the other things on their "Would Do" list, such as traveling, studying, and reading and allows them to have the things on their "Would Have" list, such as their new home and new car and other things they desire.

When you are going against the flow of the universe, you can have everything on your "Have" list, including your million dollars, and still not be rich. You have probably heard of millionaires committing suicide because they were unhappy, depressed, insecure, worried, filled with fear. Seek until you grasp the ah-hah. Having money does not cause you to be happy, but being happy can cause you to have money. In going against the flow of the universe you've always thought having things causes you to be happy but the exact opposite is true. **Being** happy may cause you to have things.

No matter which direction you are going, against the

universe or with it, you still do many of the same things. It is simply that when you are flowing with the universe there is no effort or frustration in the doing.

Let's compare becoming a veterinarian to being a veterinarian. We have a small child who is going to become a veterinarian. When someone asks him what he's going to be when he grows up, he answers, "When I grow up, I'm going to become a veterinarian." However, he knows that he's got to have an education; he's got to have a degree; he's got to have a practice; and he's got to have clients. He must have a clinic and all of these things before he can be a veterinarian. Then we see another small child and the same question is asked of him. And his answer is, "I'm a veterinarian." And with one of his dog's feet in a sling, a Band-aid on his tail, and the dog's head covered with plaster that he's made from flour and water, this child is being a veterinarian. When he's fifteen or sixteen we find him patching up one of the neighbor's cats that's been in a fight and we ask him what he's doing. His answer, "I'm being a veterinarian." Then he goes on to college and has the opportunity to do what veterinarians do, to study and learn about veterinary medicine. And without effort and frustration he ends up having his degree and a very excellent practice. When someone asks about a good veterinarian, people always say, "I'd recommend Tom, he's been a veterinarian all of his life." Haven't you heard an expression like that? Can you understand there is less effort, less frustration for the person who is being a veterinarian than for the person who has to have an education, who has to have knowledge, who has to have a degree, have an office, have equipment, have clients and all the rest before he can be a veterinarian.

Now let's really open up our awareness and understand that when we start out in **being** we are simply focusing upon that which is non-physical. We are learning to give more importance, more attention, more desire to that which is non-physical because that is the reality, the cause from which all things come.

Notice that everything we have down on our list under **being** is non-physical. It is not tangible. And that is the reality of life. We all know this. We just don't understand it. No matter how limited our knowledge of physics is, we still know that what we call physically real is only real to us in a non-physical way.

Right now you think you see this book in front of you, don't you? But the book is not really there. Where is it? For you as an individual, where is the book? In reality the book you see in front of you, you really see in your mind. What you are seeing is a bunch of light rays reflecting from the book to the retina of your eyes which is transformed to a nerve impulse and transmitted through the optic nerve to the occipital area of the brain. And there is where the book is real to you. You may say, "But I can feel the book in my hands." What you are really feeling is caused by impulses going from your hands through the neurological pathways to the brain and firing a specific brain cell pattern. You cannot call those nerve impulses nor the brain cell pattern a book. It's for this reason that I have no fear when I am speaking, whether to a small group or a convention of four or five thousand people. Do you understand why? There's nobody out there. **There is really nobody out there.** The only place the audience can be real to me is in my brain-mind functioning. That which we call physically real is a non-physical reality to our brain-mind functioning.

Since everything that we are calling physically real is only real to us in a non-physical way, let's carry this reality into a different perspective. Let's say that the real living or the real life is the non-physical life. That life which we experience after so-called death. Now as we start getting further out or further within, whichever you choose, let's keep this perspective in mind. It doesn't matter if this is real or unreal; it doesn't matter if it is true or untrue; and it doesn't matter if you believe or disbelieve it. What is important is that you might use the concept to bring more joy and peace of mind into your life. Now, in our perspective, we are saying that the real life is that non-physical life which comes after death; and to complete this perspective let's say that life is about 5,000 years long, in this part of the universe, before we go on toward the Center and the Source.

Now if you knew your life would be 5,000 years long, wouldn't you like to have a few vacations? Certainly you would. Most people can't go one year here without a vacation. So let's analyze for a moment what a vacation really is. Many people think they take their vacation for relaxation but that's not necessarily so. My favorite vacation is the first day the ski hill opens. I'm usually on the first chair when the lift opens in the morning and by noon I am exhausted. Do I quit? No, not until the lifts close at 4:30 in the afternoon and then I limp off the hill, beat, bruised, scraped, scratched, and totally exhausted. If somebody asks how did the day go, my answer is always, "Great, greatest day of the year!" You understand I would not work that hard for myself or the boss or God or anybody else and yet I call that a vacation. A vacation is really just a change.

In other words, if you take a vacation to the beach for a week and you take the typewriter and all of your office work with you, are you really taking a vacation? No, you are really just moving the office to the beach. If it is going to be a total vacation, then you must forget the office where you work, forget the job you were doing, and even forget who you were in relation to your job. If you forget who you were, where you came from, and what you were doing, it becomes a total change or a total vacation. The most important reason for the total change is so that you can go back to your job with a new perspective and really feel like getting the job done.

Most of us take little vacations from our jobs each day called coffee breaks. However, some people really take their breaks, some do not. Let's imagine four people taking their coffee break from washing dishes in a kitchen. Two of them are sitting at a table and their conversation is going something like this: "Those dishes are going to be piled all the way to the ceiling by the time we get back. They were supposed to have the hot water heater fixed yesterday, but we'll probably have to wash dishes in cold water for another week. I don't know why they can't get the air conditioner working. I bet it's 110° in the kitchen." Now, are these two people taking a break? No, they are still washing dishes.

The other two people on break are sitting at another table and their conversation goes something like this: "This weekend let's go fishing. We can take my pickup and your camp tent. Let's have the wives get all the groceries ready and we can leave Friday night. The fishing should really be good this weekend." Now are these two people taking a break? Yes, because they have forgotten who they were, what they were doing, and where they came from. They have forgotten they were dishwashers, washing dishes, in the kitchen.

An example of a total vacation might be the Mardi Gras in New Orleans. If you should ever go to the Mardi Gras and you want it to be a total vacation, a total change, then wear a costume. If you wear a costume, you may walk down the street arm-in-arm with strangers. You may walk up to total strangers and give them a hug and kiss provided they are dressed in costume also. The moment we put on a costume we start acting out the part of the costume and thus we forget who we were, where we came from, and what we were doing. Women should be especially aware of this. Don't they act differently when they are all dressed up in a cocktail gown as compared to when they are going around the house in their favorite old housecoat with their hair in curlers? Certainly they act differently, and they don't have to be reminded that they are all dressed up in a cocktail dress and so must act in a certain manner, or that they are in a housecoat and, therefore, act in a different manner.

The costume creates your act. I will never forget a masquerade dance in my home town when I was a teenager. There was one woman who was puzzled all evening by an individual in his costume. She kept saying she knew who it was but just couldn't figure it out. Do you know who it was when everyone unmasked at midnight? It was her husband. You see, when he put on the costume he started a new act which caused him to forget who he was, where he came from, and what he had been doing so completely that even his own wife did not recognize him.

The moment we put on a costume we start acting, which causes us to forget who we were, where we came from, and what we were doing, therefore, creating total change, or in other words, a perfect vacation. So let's discuss acting for a few moments. There are all kinds of acting--school plays, civic theatre, TV, movies, drama class--but basically we act for one reason. We put on an act for recognition and applause. We do not expect the applause while we are memorizing our lines, instead we usually expect ciriticism from our directors. Though once we get the act memorized if we do not get any recognition, what do we do? We change the act.

Let's also keep in mind that when we are acting, we only expect the recognition and applause from the audience. We do not expect recognition and applause from fellow actors and actresses on stage with us. In other words, just because you perform your part perfectly, you do not expect the rest of the cast on stage to applaud you.

We also enjoy every role we play. It doesn't matter whether you receive the part of the hero or the villain, the master or the maid, you enjoy acting out the role. If you played the part of the hunchback in drama class in high school, you really enjoyed being a hunchback because you received recognition and applause for your act. Fortunately, when we are acting, we realize that the character we are acting out is not really us and so when the curtain closes we stop acting. In other words, if you are acting out the part of the murderer, you don't go on killing people after the play is over. We also realize that as an actor develops his ability, he is able to act out many different roles.

There is a lot of freedom in acting but there is one rule you must always obey. As long as you are on stage, you must keep acting. If you forget your lines, then you must ad-lib. You might forget your lines and panic and faint, but as long as you are passed out on stage in front of an audience, you are still acting. Understand, that no matter what you are doing, as long as you are on stage in front of the audience, you are acting.

Let's go back now to our perspective of the real life being that non-physical life after death. Let's say that you have been living in the non-physical life after death for fifty or a hundred years--working, going to school, teaching, unemployed, drifting. No matter what you may have been doing, after fifty or a hundred years you would probably like a change. And so you plan to take a vacation and as you look around at all the vacation spots you finally decide to go to the gigantic summer theater called planet Earth.

A vacation, remember, is a change so that we may go back with a new perspective. That change happens when we forget where we came from, what we were doing, and who we were, and all we need to do to forget is to start acting. All we need to do to start acting is to

put on a costume. Planet Earth is a unique vacation
spot in that we get to create our own costume when
we come. We call it a body, and it's disposable when
we leave. This is very fortunate because think how
frustrating it would be if when you came here you had
to get inside one of the old, discarded costumes. They
would all be too big or small, too fat or skinny, or too
old or young. You might spend most of your vacation
just trying to decide upon a costume.

Your body really is a costume. It might be likened to
watching a knight in shining armor at the Mardi Gras.
We might say, "Look at his funny eyes." But they
wouldn't really be his eyes, would they? They would
be the holes in the armor in his costume that he was
looking out through. Your eyes are not really your
eyes, they are just the holes in your costume that the
real you is looking out through. We might look at the
knight and say, "Look at his funny ears," but they
wouldn't be his ears, they would simply be the holes in
his costume he listens through. And your ears are not
really your ears, they are simply the holes in your
costume which you listen through.

In this day of medical science we ought to begin to
understand that whatever we are, it is not the
physical body. Doctors can amputate both of your
arms and still you are you. They can also amputate
both legs and you are still you. They can take out one
of your kidneys and you are still you. They can give
you the blood out of some other costume and you are
still you. They can even take the heart out of some
old, worn-out costume and put it in you and you still
remain yourself. Whatever it is that is really you, it
must not be the physical body.

In this day and age there is talk about a human spare-parts bank and this may possibly be a future reality. At some point in the future, if you should rip the arm off your costume, you would simply go in and have them sew on another arm from an old discarded costume. Whatever it is that is really you, it must not be the human body.

So once you have your costume created, the spotlights go on, the curtains open, you come on stage (planet Earth), and you start acting. That's called being born and you have been acting ever since.

There are all kinds of acts. Everyone starts off with the little child act. The little child is so close to where he came from he has some idea of where he is and what it is all about and so little children are professional actors. They will change their act ten times in five minutes for recognition because they understand that is the only reason for acting. Small children understand they are only acting. Adults have lost this understanding. If a child does something stupid, another child says to him, "stop acting stupid." The adult says, "stop being stupid." If a child does something mean, another child will say to him, "stop acting mean." The adult says "stop being mean."

Adults can do beautiful things with small children if they take the perspective that the small child is a professional actor learning new acts. The adult is acting as the child's director and audience. Whether or not they are aware of it, adults are already acting out the roles of director and audience for children. Because they are not aware of this perspective, they usually give the child more recognition and applause for the things they don't want them to do rather than for the things they do want them to do. Most parents give the child more attention and recognition for not eating certain healthy foods at mealtime than for eating their meal.

Between the ages of three and five, most children begin putting on a new act at bedtime. When mother and father tell the child it's time to go to bed, the child says he doesn't want to go to bed and crawls up in the corner of the sofa with a very stubborn pout on his face. He knows this act will give him more recognition than quietly going to bed and he certainly gets the recognition. Mother and father yell at him, "If you don't go to bed right now, you are going to get a spanking." During the next TV commercial mother or father notice his act again and give the child more recognition. They drag him into the bedroom and put him in bed. Now the child is really getting recognition and he really gets into the act. He starts screaming and crying until he finally receives total recognition for the act he is putting on--mother or father applauding his bottom.

Understand, the child will put on whatever act which will give him the most recognition. If you acted out the role of the spoiled brat in drama class in high school, didn't you enjoy the recognition in the anger directed toward you from the audience? Don't you think the child enjoys the same recognition for his temper tantrum.

My children started putting on this same "I don't want to go to bed" act when they were three or four years old. I vividly recall the beginning of my oldest son's bedtime act. One night when I told him it was time to go to bed, he climbed up in the corner of the

couch, folded his arms, put a pout on his face and said
he didn't want to go to bed. Now Kay and I knew he
was only acting because we know that all children like
to sleep, so we put on the act (notice that I said **we** put
on the **act**) of ignoring his act. We know that being
ignored is the worst kind of recognition any
professional actor can receive for a good act. So Kay
and I continued with our conversation and reading
until we were ready to go to bed. As we turned out the
lights to leave the room, Trent wanted to know where
we were going. We said, "We're going to bed," and
Trent said, "Wait a minute, I want to go to bed too."

The next night he changed his act. Instead of pouting
and sitting on the couch, he stomped off to his
bedroom and cried for twenty minutes. We put on the
act of ignoring that act. A few nights later he changed
his act a little more. He stomped off to bed and cried a
few minutes and then he had to have a drink of water-
-and another and another. Now, it's O.K. with me if
he puts on that act. After all, I know his stomach will
only hold so much and if he wants to put on the act of
wetting the bed, that's O.K., too. After all, he's the
one who has to sleep in it.

Finally, one night he got into an act for which I gave
him the kind of recognition he was looking for. After
getting into bed he said, "Daddy, come here. I want to
tell you something." As the child's director and
audience, we are always interested in any new role
they begin learning. So I went into the bedroom and
asked, "What do you want to tell me?" And he
answered, "Daddy, I love you." Now I know that is
just an act, too, but I feel putting on the act of love is
going to give the child a lot more happiness as he goes

through life than putting on the act of the temper
tantrum. So I applauded his act and we sat down and
talked about love for four or five minutes.

The next night he changed his whole act. He ran into
the bedroom, jumped into bed, pulled the covers up
and then said, "Daddy, come here, I want to tell you
something." I asked what about and he said, "I love
you." And so we talked about his loving daddy and
daddy loving him and I started to leave. Then he said,
"Wait a minute, I want to tell you something else. I
love mommy, too." And so we spent some more time
talking about love. Finally, he developed the act to the
point where he looked forward to going to bed and
talking to mommy and daddy about love. He loved
mommy and daddy and his brother and all of his
playmates and teachers. He loved the trees and the
sky and God and the grass and the insects and day and
night. He spent a great deal of time during the day
seeing things to love so that he might put on the act of
staying awake another twenty minutes at bedtime. I
knew it was an act, but usually the act of love results
in more happiness as we go through life, so I
applauded him for the act. The reason children like to
put on an act at bedtime which will give them a lot of
recognition is because they know they are going to be
sleeping for eight or ten hours with no audience and
no recognition and so like all professional actors, they
like a few encores at the end of a day's performance.

Understand, the little child will put on whatever act
you give them the most recognition for. If you will
look closely at what the child is and what he is doing
today, you will understand that what he is and what
he is doing is what he has received the most

recognition for. We see two small children playing quietly together for two hours and then they have a three minute quarrel, and they receive more recognition for their three minute act of quarreling than they did for their two hour act of playing quietly. Naturally, these children are going to perfect the act of quarreling. Many children receive a one sentence compliment in recognition for their act of making an "A" on their report card and receive an hour lecture in recognition for making a "D." Naturally, they perfect the act of making a "D." It gives them greater recognition.

Since a small child is spending nearly all of his time learning new acts, he, of course, can change his act easier than an adult. A beautiful example of this was a speech therapist who had gone through this Results Training, and in turn spent a half-hour talking to a nine-year-old child about the act he was putting on of not talking intelligibily. She explained to him that the act was O.K., and he would always receive special recognition for it. Other children would act like they didn't like him; they would act like he was crazy. He would probably receive a lot of "F's" from his teachers for his act. Later on coaches may not want him to play first string in any sports. If he graduated from school, many companies wouldn't want to hire him because of his act. She explained all of the probable recognition he would receive for acting like he could not talk but that it was perfectly O.K. to act that way. She told him that any time he wantd to change, he could start acting like he could talk clearly and that would be O.K., too.

And then she explained the kind of recognition he

might receive for talking clearly. More children would want to play with him and be friends. It would be easier for him to make passing grades and make it easier for him to participate in all the activities and sports that he wanted to. When he graduated from school he would probably get a higher paying job so he could buy his own car or whatever else he wanted.

Five minutes after the child had left the room, another teacher came to the therapist and wanted to know what she had done to the child because for the first time the child had walked into her classroom and started speaking intelligibily enough to understand.

You see, the speech therapist simply pointed out to the child the recognition he would receive for talking clearly and the child decided he would rather have the recognition for talking clearly and totally changed his act in five minutes.

We should also understand recognition or applause is in the tone of our voice, the expression of our face, our body movements, our feelings and our emotions, as well as the words we say.

The next act we progress into is the teenage act. The difference between a teenager and an adult is that adults have their acts so well memorized that they never forget a line and so everybody applauds them for their acts. Teenagers are still memorizing their acts and so naturally now and then they forget one of their lines and each time they do there seems to be an adult around to tell them they are wrong. Teenagers have been here long enough, though, that adults have convinced them that it is not an act, that their hang-ups are real. This has caused one of the most destructive teenage acts in many years. The new teenage act that is going around is the act of not acting. It is the teenager who is saying, "All adults are false, they are acting, but not me. I'm just being myself!" Do you see the slavery in this? If what you are doing right now is just being you, then that is all you can do the rest of your life. If you don't know you are acting when the curtain falls and the scene is finished, you will go on acting out the same role. If you take the perspective that whatever you are doing is simply an act, then you have the freedom to learn a new manuscript at any time you desire.

I really enjoy watching teenagers go through this training. Because teenagers haven't got their acts completely memorized, they may change their acts easier than adults when they take the perspective that it is all an act. A beautiful example was a seventeen-year-old girl, a senior in high school, who had never dated. She had never dated because she had developed her act of shyness to perfection. She had developed her act of shyness so well that if a boy spoke to her she became tongue-tied and could not talk to him. Everybody who knew her gave her applause for her shy act. Her parents, her brothers and sisters, her girl friends, they all kept telling her how shy she was, until the only way she could be right was by acting shy.

When this girl attended this training she grasped the perspective that she was not really shy, instead, she was only acting shy. Her first question was, "How do I change my act?" The answer is simple. There are hundreds of books written with advice on how to develop an outgoing personality. If you don't choose to study books, then simply watch some actresses who have perfected the act of an open, outgoing personality and start mimicking them. Watch how they walk and talk, laugh and giggle. Listen to their jokes and conversations with boys and then simply start acting in the same manner. You will naturally forget a few of your lines while you are learning this new manuscript, but as soon as you have it memorized all of the boys will applaud you. This girl chose to learn her new act through mimicking her girl friends who already had the act perfected. It was only a matter of two or three weeks until she was getting applause from many of the boys and going out on dates.

Then one day catastrophe befell her and she came to me in tears explaining what had happened. She'd had a crush on a boy in her class since the seventh grade but she had never spoken to him. The day before she talked with me he had stopped her in the hall at school and started talking to her. She said everything was going great with her new act until he asked her for a date. At that point she forgot all of her new lines and could not even speak a word. Finally, he just walked off shaking his head thinking she was crazy and through her tears she wailed, "I know he will never ask me out again." I explained to her that in this perspective this boy was simply acting as her audience and even though the audience is the first to criticize you when you forget your lines, they are also the first to applaud you when you have them perfected. With this perspective, she faithfully went back to memorizing her new act and do you know who she started going steady with? Yes, the boy she'd had a crush on since seventh grade.

Understand in using this perspective you are putting on just as big an act in making an "A" as you are making an "F" and neither one is good or bad. It is simply that they have different results. If you take the perspective that both success and failure are an act, then you have the freedom to memorize either one. It is easier and takes less time to memorize the success manuscript than it does the failure manuscript. This is simply because there is a lot more competition in the failure act. In other words, a lot more people are putting on the failure act than the success act. If you want to fail, you really have to be an expert because there is a lot of competition. There are not as many people putting on the success act and so there is not much competition, consequently, the manuscript is not nearly so thick and difficult to learn. Unfortunately, many youth receive more recognition and applause from their family, their teachers, and other youth for the act of failure than they do for the act of success.

We have had fantastic success in opening up this perspective with the mentally and emotionally handicapped. We explain that they are simply putting on a mentally handicapped act which is certainly O.K. in every respect. We point out to them the kind of recognition and applause they will probably receive for putting on that act for the rest of their lives. Then we explain the "normal act," if there is such a thing, and the type of recognition and applause they may receive for it. We make it clear that either act is O.K., whether they remain with their mentally handicapped act or learn the new normal act. It is their choice, not ours. With this perspective many have changed their act within a few weeks.

Your thoughts are the manuscripts of your acts. When you think the same kind of thoughts again and again, it will eventually become a predominant brain cell pattern. Your predominant brain cell patterns are your habits, and your habits are your acts. For your acts you receive recognition from yourself and other people. If you like the recognition, you think the act is good. If you don't like the recognition, you think the act is bad. It will be easier to change your acts if you understand it is not the act which you like or dislike. It is the recognition you are getting from yourself or other people which you like or dislike. If a person bites his fingernails, he does not dislike the act of biting fingernails. He loves biting his fingernails. What he dislikes is the recognition he gets for biting his nails. If a person smokes, he does not dislike the act of smoking. He enjoys smoking, but he dislikes the recognition he gets from himself and other people for the act. Understand, if you are acting lazy, you enjoy the lazy act. You just don't like people telling you about it.

What people like or dislike about their acts is the recognition they receive; therefore, the best way to help someone change their act is in the kind of recognition you give them. When someone desires to change an act, give them an abundance of recognition and applause for that desire. Also give them an abundance of applause every time they rehearse any part of the new act.

When you haven't got your role completely memorized, then you feel like you're acting. When you have the role memorized and it becomes a habit, you think it's your nature. You have heard people make the comment that they can't stand a certain person because they're always acting and not being themselves. That person is simply memorizing a new role. Once they have memorized the new role, it will seem like a natural part of them.

The next acts we progress into are the adult acts. Unfortunately, adults are programmed that only youth are acting; whatever adults do is real. Adults started acting when they were born and they are still acting and they are enjoying their acts even more now because they have them better memorized and are getting more recognition. Remember when we discussed acting, we agreed that no matter what act we put on we enjoy it. This means if you are putting on the act of being an alcoholic today, you are enjoying it just as much as you did if you played the part of an alcoholic in drama class in high school. Unfortunately, if you are putting on the act today as an adult, you are enjoying it even more because you have the lines better memorized and so you are getting more applause.

We have all kinds of adult acts--from the hypochondriac to the health nut, from the bum to the millionaire, from the happy to the depressed, the success to the failure, the act of being a minister to the act of being a convict.

There is one very beautiful but very destructive act that many adults get into and this is the act of being needed. The act that believes, "I am happy if people need me." If people need you, they have a problem. If you are happy being needed, you are happy when other people have problems. An example might be a young married couple where the wife is putting on the act of being needed. She is very happy in this act because she is supporting her husband while he is going through college and he really needs her. And after he finishes college, he decides to go through medical school and she is still happy feeling needed. After medical school there is internship. And even when he starts his practice, she is needed to support him until his practice builds.

Then one day she panics, her husband has a very successful practice supporting the family well and she no longer feels needed. In her desperation she will cause something to happen. She may get her husband on alcohol or raise children with hang-ups; she will do something to bring problems into her environment so she can feel needed again.

Understand that if other people need you, that means they must have hang-ups or problems. It is a beautiful thing to help people because they need your help. It is a whole different world to help people because it makes you feel needed. Please understand that we are not talking about the acts like **needing help or wanting to help,** but rather the act of **needing to be needed.** It is a beautiful thing to help people because you want to help them, but not because it makes you feel needed.

The reason there are so many different acts is because there are many different types of vacations and different vacations create different acts. Perhaps you have talked with someone who was taking a week's vacation from work and when you asked them what they were going to do, the answer was something like, "I am going to buy me some beer and go home and sit and watch TV and drink beer and forget about my job for a week." Now isn't that a good way to forget where you came from, what you were doing, and who you were in relation to your job so that you might go back to work with a new and fresh perspective? Well, a lot of people have come to planet Earth on the same vacation. These people didn't come to do anything. They just came to see the sights and watch what's going on and everybody else is trying to save them. They are already doing what they came for, so perhaps we should spend more time saving ourselves.

Someone else may take a vacation with no plans whatsoever. When you ask them where they are going on vacation, they tell you they don't know. They have everything loaded in the car and they are taking off in the morning and wherever they go and whatever they do will be great. Now isn't that an O.K. vacation to forget where you came from and what you were doing in relation to your job, which will allow you to go back to your job with a new perspective. A lot of people come to planet Earth on that kind of vacation--just doing whatever happens and everyone is trying to save them. I constantly have people telling me that certain friends of theirs just don't seem to care because whatever happens is O.K. These people are doing what they came for. Instead of worrying about them, perfect your own vacation.

If I should have the opportunity to come back to Earth on vacation again, I many times think I would like to come back as a profoundly retarded human vegetable. I don't know about you, but my mind seems to go full speed constantly and every now and then I would like to turn it all off for a few hours. I don't mean through meditation or by going to sleep and dreaming, I mean totally shutting it off and isn't that kind of what the human vegetable is doing. Now, wouldn't it really freak you out, if a few years after I have finished this vacation, you were going through the hospital looking at all the poor helpless human vegetables, and about that time one rolled over and winked at you and said, "Hi, I'm Wally." The perspective I gain from this idea is that my teacher in the other dimension might possibly be the bum on skid row in this dimension. I am quite sure my teachers in the non-physical dimension might just want to sit and watch TV and drink beer when they get their vacation and forget all about teaching Wally. This perspective allows me to look into the costume and see the inner perfection in every person no matter what act they are putting on.

There are also people who take a vacation with everything planned in minute detail. Maybe they have planned to go to the coast for a week. They have planned the exact route, the motels they will stay in, the times they will go fishing. Their vacation is all planned in complete detail. But it just happens, when they reach the top of the coastal range of mountains, their car breaks down. When they take the car into the garage, the mechanic tells them it will take a week to fix it. Now, they have several choices. They may take everything out of the car and set it beside the road and hitchhike on their planned vacation, or they may decide that since they have been detoured they will have a beautiful vacation hiking, camping, and fishing in the mountains instead, or they may do like most people do and moan and groan for a week complaining that their whole vacation has been ruined.

Many people have come to planet Earth on a specifically planned vacation and some of them have been detoured. Now they have the same choices. They can find the means to continue on their planned vacation, or they may have a beautiful vacation where they are instead, or they may sit around and complain that planet Earth is a mess and life is not worth living.

There are also people who take vacations to learn. Many people have taken a week vacation to go through Alpha Awareness Training for a learning experience. There are people who take a whole year's vacation to go back to college for learning. There are many people who come to planet Earth on a learning vacation. They are called seekers. If you are on a learning vacation, then understand your message. The message is seek and you shall find. You see, seeking indicates a continuing process that never stops and that is what learning is all about. If you are on a trip of learning, it never stops. If you don't understand this, you are always looking for **the answer.** You have the feeling that you will find **the answer** in the next book, or the next class, the next job, the next city, the next friend, the next marriage. Understand, that if you are a seeker, there is no **"the answer."** The answer is continual learning.

Some people take vacations for danger and excitement, such as mountain climbing, sky diving, bull fighting and many other dangerous experiences. There are a lot of people who come to planet Earth for a vacation of excitement and danger, and because of this, we have things like the war game. We don't have wars because of disagreements and misunderstandings, we have wars because there are people who like to play the war game. It really is an exciting and fun game. If you don't believe this, watch the little children. What is one of their favorite games? "Bang, bang, bang--you're dead." If you really want to make the war game exciting, you do what? You go into the front line action (acting). The war act is an O.K. act, especially if you are here on a short vacation. It is a good way to get back on time.

Understand that all of the different plays going on on planet Earth are O.K. The only problem is we don't have this vacation spot completely organized. Someday we will get it organized like Disneyland. If you go to Disneyland and you want to take the jungle trip, you don't have to worry about flying saucers attacking and getting into the act. And if you want to get into the flying saucer act, you don't have to worry about an Indian shooting you. If you want to get into the cowboy and Indian act, you don't have to worry about Alice in Wonderland fouling you up. You see, in Disneyland they have a separate stage for each different play and so the actors don't foul each other up. One day maybe we can get this vacation spot, planet Earth, organized in the same manner. We will take some island, like Greenland or Australia, and divide it right in the middle and then put one half of the people who want to play the war game on one side and half on the other side. Each time a side loses an actor, they will get the next person who comes here on vacation to play the war game. This way those who come to play the war game can play it without involving any other people in their act. You see, until we get it organized, we have to have things like the draft system and when someone doesn't come to play the war game and they get drafted, naturally, they are going to complain. One day maybe we'll get it organized like Disneyland and we can have a special stage for the war game, another stage for monopoly, another stage for chess, and so on. Then each person can act in the play of their choice without being fouled up by someone else putting on a completely different act on their stage. In this perspective we might think of planet Earth as being a gigantic theater with many different stages and different plays going on simultaneously.

Now let's keep our perspective in mind that it doesn't matter if all that we have talked about is true or untrue. It's important that we don't concern ourselves with believing or disbelieving. It's kind of like thinking of your job as a hobby. What is the result? Certainly you will enjoy your job more, be more productive, and be less exhausted after a day's work. However, this is not really true. Your job is not a hobby but if you think of it as a hobby you certainly change your results. So keep this perspective in mind, that these concepts are not for believing or disbelieving but only for using to bring more happiness and peace of mind into your life.

If you are somewhat confused at this time, you are in the right space because out of confusion comes understanding. In the next part of this book we will strive to gain some enlightenment from our confusion.

THE UNIVERSE FLOWS

Having	Doing	Being
Physical	Mental	Spiritual
Least Powerful	Less Powerful	Most Powerful
Conscious	Inner Conscious	Unconscious
EGO + Imagination + Awareness	IMAGINATION + Awareness	AWARENESS
Against the Flow	EGO + Imagination + Awareness	AWARENESS
Physical Space	Mental Space	Spiritual Space
Action	Association - Evaluation - Decision	Creation
Result	Effect	Cause
Results of Love	Love Expressed	Love Is
Perform → Receive Recognition	Learn Act	Probable Acts
Comfort Zone → Problem Answer $20,000 or $25,000	View Act from Different Perspectives	Awareness of Another Act
It is all an Act So it is all Perfect	All Roles are Perfect	Probabilities are Perfect
Act Without Decision	See Perfection	The Inner-Self Perfect
Inner-Self – Audience	Inner-Self – Director	Inner-Self – Agent

THE TRUTH SHALL SET YOU FREE-THE TRUTH IS

Through a Physical Body in a Physical World	Using Mind To Express	You are a Spiritual Being (Human)

PART III

Now, let's put all this together in a manner in which we might gain enlightenment from our confusion. To gain the enlightenment from the rest of this book you need to read it several times until you can perceive all of the different parts as a whole. To help you follow more closely, you might want to refer to the chart titled, "The Universe Flows," on page **96**.

Let's focus on the areas of being, doing, and having and be aware that each one of these areas is a whole dimension in itself. In flowing with the universe the whole dimension of being flows into the dimension of doing, and that flows into the dimension of having.

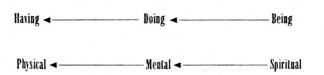

These three dimensions are also the spiritual dimension, mental dimension, and the physical dimension an these three dimensions form the foundation of your being. These three dimensions are like a tripod, one leg being the spiritual, one leg the mental, and one leg being the physical and you are a triune balanced on top of this foundation. In other words, whether or not you are aware of it, you are a spiritual, mental, physical being, which is the sum total of your experience in these three dimensions.

If you understand that you are a triune, a total of your experience in these three dimensions, then you can understand the balance of life. You can understand what causes happiness, and how peace of mind and inner peace are achieved.

Because most people are going against the flow of the universe, they spend most of their time growing in the physical dimension, the dimension of having. All of their time and effort put into the physical dimension causes the physical leg of the foundation to grow faster than the mental and spiritual legs of the foundation, and as it grows, they have more physical experiences and physical things, and the more they end up having in the physical dimension, the more they get involved in the physical world. This would be great if you could spend every moment of your life in the physical dimension, but this vacation is physical, mental, and spiritual, all at the same time. The result is that all of this growth in the physical leg of the tripod causes your foundation of life to be off balance and you find yourself toppling, hanging onto life. When an individual is mostly involved in the physical dimension, he feels like he is missing something in life. He is. He's missing the mental and spiritual growth, but because he is so physically oriented, he starts seeking more things in the physical dimension to satisfy this desire, and this creates even greater frustration--the feeling that he is not fulfilling his life.

A person may experience what we think of as positive or negative growth in any of the dimensions. In the physical dimension a person may experience growth in abundance, wealth, health, success, or they may experience growth in poverty, illness, accidents, debts, those things which we think of as being negative. At one time or another you have probably experienced your debts growing. However, when you have greater growth in any dimension you will experience more happiness in that dimension whether the growth is positive or negative.

When an individual is going against the flow of the universe, they are totally focused upon having--the physical leg of the foundation of life and their growth will usually be a negative growth. This person will usually have more problems and fewer answers because most of the answers come from the mental dimension. This person will usually have more poverty, illness, accidents, failure, and so on. However, he will still experience greater happiness when he's involved in the physical dimension.

People do experience happiness from their poverty, illness, their accidents, or their failure. A person who has had ten major operations gets a lot more happiness talking about his illnesses than a person who has only had a tonsillectomy. A person who has had several major accidents gets more happiness talking about his accidents than the person who has only had a sprained ankle. A person who has hundreds of problems gets more happiness in talking about his problems than a person who only has one or two problems. If you don't believe this, then just watch these people closely while they are telling you about their operations or accidents or problems. These people actually come alive, they really get excited, when they are talking about their illnesses or accidents or problems. You will find it nearly impossible to change the subject and after they have finished telling you about their last ten operations or accidents, they will start telling you about the next one they are going to have. People actually do experience happiness from their problems. Even as a person can experience happiness in the struggle of a football game while they are losing, so can a person experience happiness in the struggle of living while they are losing.

Another individual may spend nearly all of his time and effort growing in the mental dimension; more knowledge, more learning, more education, or in a negative manner with more worry, more depression, more fear, more guilt. As he experiences this growth in the mental dimension without equal growth in the physical or spiritual dimension, he again pushes his life off balance. Now realize that he, too, experiences greater happiness when he is totally involved in the mental dimension--when learning, when he is involved in intellectual discussions or when he is depressed or experiencing fear or worry or guilt. But because he is lacking in the physical and spiritual dimensions, he constantly has the feeling that something is missing in his life. He then usually tries to fill this vacuum by more involvement in the mental dimension--by seeking more knowledge, more education, or becoming more depressed. He goes through life without ever experiencing the peace of mind that is obtained in the balance of growth in all three dimensions.

A person who has most of his growth in the mental dimension without equal growth in the physical and spiritual dimensions usually has the answers but creates problems because he doesn't apply those answers in the physical dimension. Because they see more answers in the mental dimension but do not know how to apply them in the physical dimension, they tend to create more worry and fear and depression. Because this person does not have equal growth in the physical dimension, he usually experiences lack and poverty because material things come through the physical dimension. A person who is focused totally in the mental dimension experiences more fear, worry, and depression because the politicains and ministers and leaders of the world are not doing what this person knows should be done. However, he gets a lot of happiness out of talking about the problems and answers and criticizing the rest of the world for not doing what he sees as an answer.

There are individuals who have equal growth in the mental and physical legs of the foundation of their triune, but because they are ignoring their spiritual growth and the spiritual leg of the foundation, they still find themselves unbalanced. They still find themselves seeking and searching for that something in life that must be satisfied. Now it's true, again, they experience a greater happiness when they are involved in either the mental or physical dimension, but because of lack of growth in the spiritual leg, they still find themselves constantly searching and seeking for peace of mind. Can you understand that happiness, your greater happiness in life, is growth in any area of the triune, but your peace of mind depends upon the balance of growth.

A person who has had greater growth in the mental and physical legs of the foundation is usually the person we think of as being very successful. He tends to see the answers to his problems in the mental dimension and applies them in the physical dimension, thereby creating a lot of abundance in his life. This person will experience a lot of happiness while he is solving problems and when he is involved with all of the physical, material things he has, but he does not experience a joy of living because he is missing his sprritual growth.

As I said before, you can experience happiness while playing a football game even when you are losing but you don't experience real joy when you lose even if you only lose by one point. The experience of real joy only comes with winning. In the same way, you can experience a lot of happiness in the game of living even when you are losing, but you cannot experience total joy in life when something is missing. You experience joy in the game of living when you are winning, when you are balanced in all three dimensions.

You have also seen individuals freak themselves out in the spiritual dimension. They spend nearly all of their time in prayer, meditation, seeking spiritual enlightenment, and because of this, they have tremendous happiness when they are experiencing in the spiritual dimension. But the moment they are pushed back into the mental or physical world, they are very uncomfortable. It seems unreal to them. This is why you see many beautifully spiritually enlightened people withdraw from the world. They spend their lives in seclusion. Many of these individuals think they have truly found inner peace, peace of mind, but it is an illusion because they only experience that inner peace when they are functioning in the spiritual world. They are not able to experience inner peace when they are experiencing their total vacation, when they are experiencing the spiritual, mental, and physcial world all at once.

If an individual has the majority of his growth in the spiritual dimension, he tends to create a lack in physical material things and has difficulty in putting his ideas from the mental dimension into practical application. This individual has a tendency to see the whole but forgets the part. This person may spend so much time and energy saving the whole world that he forgets himself and ends up in poverty and illness.

You might know certain individuals and ask yourself how they can live in such total peace. They don't have anything in the physical dimension. They don't have a home; they don't have nice clothes; they don't have a car. They don't have much development in the mental dimension either. They don't have an education; they don't do a lot of thinking; they don't really use their brain-mind functioning. They also lack development in the spiritual dimension. They don't meditate; they don't pray. They don't have a religion, and yet they continually live with peace of mind. You see, their tripod may only be a few inches high, but it's balanced in all three areas. They may never experience truly great happiness in life, but they are able to experience peace of mind. They have inner peace because of their balance in all three dimensions.

It is very simple to control the growth for your greater happiness and the balance for your peace of mind as you go through life. Whenever you find yourself in a period where you are hanging onto life, when life seems unfulfilled and a part of your life seems empty, then analyze the trip you are on. Usually you will find out that you have been involved in just one dimension, either physical or mental or spiritual. If you have been on a mental trip, a trip of more knowledge or learning, more education or more worry and depression, then simply take some time to get involved in the physical world. Take a day and go hiking or fishing. Get out and work in the yard, mow the lawn, do some physical labor and then balance that time in the spiritual dimension. Spend some time praying, meditating, seeking spiritual enlightenment and very quickly you will find your life in balance again and you will enjoy living.

One method of accomplishing this balance is to always keep yourself involved in a project in each dimension. Perhaps your job is in the physical dimension, physical labor. Then you should also get involved in some project in the mental dimension. Get into some educational classes or set aside a certain amount of time each week for reading educational material. Get involved in some project that constantly expands your intellect. Become involved in projects that expand your spiritual understanding: reading, discussion groups, prayer, meditation, classes-- whatever seems best for you as an individual. Constantly being involved in all three dimensions in this manner will keep your life in balance, and you will experience peace of mind as well as happiness and joy.

As we go on, keep this formula in mind: greater growth in any dimension--spiritual, mental or physical--equals greater happiness in that dimension. Balanced growth in all three dimensions equals peace and joy.

To keep this balance, this inner peace, you must realize that the spiritual dimension is the most powerful dimension, the mental dimension is less powerful, and the physical dimension is the least powerful. Mull this over in your mind and mentally digest it, because if you don't understand this, you may find yourself freaked out in the spiritual dimension. You probably already realize that each dimension is equally important, and so it may seem that you need to spend equal time in each dimension for equal growth. But because the spiritual dimension is the most powerful and the mental dimension less powerful, you may spend minutes in the spiritual dimension and experience the same amount of growth that would take hours to experience in the mental dimension. And because the physical dimension is the least powerful, you may have to spend days in the physical dimension to have the same amount of growth. Because the spiritual dimension is the most powerful, you may spend minutes in meditation or prayer and become aware of something that would take you hours in the mental dimension to understand and then take days in the physical dimension to act out.

Perhaps if we could get a better understanding of the

oneness of these three dimensions we could better understand how the spiritual dimension is the most powerful. Even though the spiritual dimension, the mental dimension, and the physical dimension are each separate realities on their own, they all three occupy the same space at the same time, and all three come from the same source. You should understand this because many times the line that divides these three dimensions is so fine that it seems to be non-existent.

Let's say we have a five gallon bucket and we fill the space in this bucket with large glass crystal balls. Now these crystal balls will represent the physical dimension, the dimension of having. And now let's take glass marbles, which represent the mental dimension, your imagination, the dimension of doing, and pour the marbles into the five gallon bucket which is already filled with crystal balls. As we shake the bucket around a bit, the marbles filter down through the crystal balls. Now we have the same space occupied by both crystal balls and marbles at the same time. Now, let's take sand crystals, which represent the spiritual dimension, your awareness, the dimension of being, and pour the sand into the five gallon bucket which is already filled with crystal balls and marbles. As we shake the bucket around, the sand filters down through the crystal balls and marbles. Now we have the space in the five gallon bucket filled with crystal balls (the physical dimension) and marbles (the mental dimension) and sand (the spiritual dimension) all at the same time.

Now if you were to close your eyes and reach into the bucket and take something out, you would probably come up with a crystal ball. And you would say that the space is filled with crystal balls. In this same manner, as you go through life, you are more aware of the physical, the tangible, what you have, than you are of the mental dimension, the imagination. So you tend to think that your physical dimension is the most important because it is the most tangible. We tend to think that having is more important than knowing. In fact, our greatest motivation for knowing more in the mental dimension is so that we can have more in the physical dimension. But if you were to take all of the crystal balls out of the bucket, you would then realize that there are many more marbles in that space than there were crystal balls. In this manner of comparison the mental dimension is more powerful than the physical dimension.

Now, if, after all the crystal balls are removed, you again closed your eyes and reached into the bucket and took something out, you would probably take out a marble and you would think the space is filled with marbles. Just as marbles are easier to be aware of than grains of sand, you have the tendency to think your mental dimension, your knowledge, is more important than your spiritual dimension. People tend to think that knowing something is more important than understanding it. You probably know how your family members and close friends will act under given conditions but do you understand why they act that way? If we would understand our friends and family as well as we know them, we would have truly beautiful relationships.

After you removed all the marbles from the space, you would then realize that there are many, many more grains of sand in that space than there were marbles. As there are many, many more grains of sand than marbles, so is your spiritual dimension more powerful than your mental dimension.

Realize that all three are just as important and that all three occupy the same space at the same time, but as there are more grains of sand, which represent the spiritual dimension, your awareness, your being, that dimension is the most powerful. In that same space there are fewer marbles, which represent the mental dimension, your imagination, your doing, and so that dimension is less powerful. In that space there are even fewer crystal balls, which represent the physical dimension, your ego, your having, and so that dimension is the least powerful.

Now circle closely so that you may receive another ah-hah. What are glass marbles made of? They are made of sand crystals. And what are crystal balls made of? Yes, they, too, are made of sand crystals. You see, even though the spiritual dimension, the mental dimension, and the physical dimension are separate realities, they all three occupy the same space at the same time and, even more important, all three come from the same source. It is for these same reasons the fine, thin line dividing these dimensions many times seems to be non-existent.

As you continue reading you might think of yourself in comparison to the bucket. Think of yourself as a physical, mental, spiritual being all in one, and your mental self and physical self coming from your spiritual self.

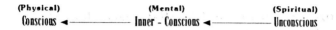

(Physical)	(Mental)	(Spiritual)
Conscious ◄————————	Inner - Conscious ◄————————	Unconscious

As we go on now, let's relate these three dimensions to the mind. Unconscious mind is in the spiritual dimension, inner-conscious* or subconscious mind is in the mental dimension, and conscious mind is in the physical dimension. As we look at these three areas of the mind in perspective to their respective dimensions, let's understand that we are not human beings but rather we are being human during the short time we are on this vacation. You see, what we think of ourselves as human beings is pretty much limited to what we perceive through the conscious function of our mind, which is the least powerful part, and a little bit of what we perceive through the subconscious part of our mind. If we just stop a moment and become aware, then we must understand that this is only a small part of us. We know that even while we are awake, our subconscious and unconscious mind is constantly working, doing things that we couldn't possibly do with our conscious mind, such as keeping our heart beating, digesting food, and growing new cells. And then, there is that whole one-third of our life we spend asleep; when the conscious mind turns off and the subconscious and unconscious mind keep working with total control. With this awareness, can't we get our conscious ego to accept that the greater, more powerful part of our reality is that part of us that we are so unaware of, that part of us that we seldom even think of as being

*Refer to ALPHA AWARENESS TRAINING BOOK.

human? Yes, the truth is, that which we call a human being is mostly a non-physical reality. The truth is that we are being a little bit human, using mind to express through a physical body in a physical world.

Now you may say, "How can we ever function in the spiritual dimension if it is in the unconscious area of mind?" If you have read the book ALPHA AWARENESS TRAINING* or participated in an Alpha Awareness class, that is what a lot of the training was really about, bringing these areas of your mind into balance so that you can begin to experience inner peace. Prior to your Alpha Awareness Training, your awareness was focused almost totally in the conscious area of mind, which, being so close to the subconscious mind, allowed information to constantly filter through from the subconscious into your conscious awareness. Through Alpha Awareness Training you learn to focus more awareness in the inner-conscious or sub-conscious mind. This area of mind is so close to the unconscious area it allows more of your unconscious experience to filter through to your awareness. This then creates a natural balance of the three dimensions and because the spiritual dimension is the most powerful, seconds in the spiritual dimension are equal to minutes in the mental dimension and hours in the physical dimension.

We might better understand the unconscious, subconscious and conscious parts of mind by discussing the predominant faculties of our brain-

*The ALPHA AWARENESS TRAINING BOOK teaches you how to function with awareness in your subconscious mind in your normal waking state and therefore is an extremely valuable tool in totally understanding this RESULTS BOOK. (Order forms on pages 172-173.)

mind functioning through which we relate to each dimension.

(Physical)   (Mental)   (Spiritual)

EGO + Imagination + Awareness ◄– IMAGINATION + Awareness ◄———— AWARENESS

Awareness is the predominant faculty through which we relate to the spiritual dimension. Imagination is the predominant faculty through which we relate to the mental dimension, and ego is the predominant faculty through which we relate to the physical dimension.

Awareness is a recognition of what is. Awareness in the spiritual dimension deals primarily with the recognition of future possibilities or probabilities.

Imagination, the predominant faculty through which we relate to the mental dimension, is the mental process of association and evaluation. Whenever we perceive anything, through the physical senses or extrasensory awareness or any other form of perception, the imagination immediately associates this information with any similar information previously impressed upon brain cells. After the process of association the imagination will evaluate the information. The evaluation is primarily based on the similar information previously impressed on brain cells and, therefore, any decision we make may have very little to do with what is happening in the present moment.

If you perceive your child having a temper tantrum, you immediately associate it with previous temper tantrums and previous decisions you have made about the child's tantrums. You may associate it with books you have read on advice about tantrums and what other people have suggested to you about tantrums. Then you will evaluate the present temper tantrum based partially or totally upon this previous information. Therefore, your decision is going to be based on previous information and may have very little to do with the present temper tantrum. Both the process of association and evaluation deal primarily with the past. Therefore, much of our imagination deals with the past.

As the universe flows from being into doing into having, so does awareness flow from the spiritual dimension into the mental dimension and functions there with the imagination. Awareness functioning with the imagination in the mental dimension relates the past to the future and recognizes future possibilities. In other words, if you have awareness working with your imagination when you are associating and evaluating the temper tantrums, through awareness you might recognize a new and different approach to the temper tantrum. When you are going against the flow of the universe, you are blocking most of your awareness of future possibilities out of the mental dimension. If you do not have your awareness working with imagination, you will react to the temper tantrum from your past experience.

Ego, the predominant faculty of the brain-mind functioning through which we relate to the physical dimension, is defined by the dictionary as "that part of the personality that is conscious and most in touch with the external reality." Ego is that part of your personality which compares yourself. Ego is the part of the personality which judges. Being the predominant control factor of the physical dimension, ego should be used mainly to compare the act we are putting on with the recognition or the result we are getting from the act. Ego in the physical dimension is that faculty which relates the present to the past and the future. Therefore, the ego deals predominantly with the present. As the universe flows from the spiritual into the mental into the physical, so do awareness and the imagination flow into the physical dimension and function with the ego. Imagination, functioning in the physical dimension, relates the past to the present moment. Awareness, functioning in the physical dimension, relates the future to the present moment. When you are flowing with the universe, you have awareness, imagination and ego all working together in the physical dimension, and you are able to arrive at better decisions about how to act in the present.

We might, in a sense, think of awareness and imagination and ego as being the predominant control factors of each dimension. Awareness would be the predominant control factor through which we relate to the spiritual dimension; imagination, the predominant control factor through which we relate to the mental dimension; and ego, the predominant control factor through which we relate to the physical dimension.

Ego in its own dimension, the area of having, the physical dimension, is so natural we don't even recognize it as ego. When a professional ski racer wins a race, what is the predominant factor that causes him to win? It's ego. It's that part of the conscious personality which compares itself to the external or the outer reality. It's that part of the personality which compares the act with the recognition or the result of the act and causes us to say, "I can do better. I can go faster. I have perfect balance. I have perfect control. I can win." And when the skier comes through the finish line first we all applaud him. We don't think he is on an ego trip because he won the race. It is only when we get ego into the mental dimension that we have egotism. Let's say this skier is being interviewed after he wins the race. An interview is communication and communication is predominantly in the mental dimension. If the skier is flowing with the universe, he allows his imagination to be the control factor in the interview. When he's asked how he won the race, he says, "I won the race because I love winning, because I enjoy practicing and improving my skiing. I won the race because I love the excitement and the speed on the ski hill." And when the interview is finished, we applaud him again.

(Physical)	**(Mental)**	**(Spiritual)**
Against the Flow ----- ►	EGO + Imagination + Awareness --------- ►	Awareness

Most individuals are constantly going against the flow of the universe. They are constantly going from having into doing into being. If you are going against the universe from the physical into the mental into the spiritual, then you are also forcing your ego to function in the mental dimension. This pushing against the flow of the universe and getting ego in the mental dimension is what causes many of our problems in life.

Let's say we have another skier who became a professional skier going against the flow of the universe. He started out having all the things skiers have and then doing what skiers do, and finally becoming a skier. Going against the universe causes his ego to function in the mental dimension. After this skier wins the race, he is interviewed, but instead of imagination being the predominant control factor, ego becomes his predominant control factor in the mental dimension. And so when he is asked how he won the race, his reply is, "I won the race because I am the greatest skier in the world. My competitors are a bunch of bums. They should still be on the bunny hill. They don't know how to ski. I am better than they are so naturally I won the race." When his interview is finished we no longer applaud him, do we? You see, because he got ego involved in the mental dimension, he's experiencing what we call egotism. He becomes an egotist. Allowing ego to become the control factor in the mental dimension causes an ego trip, and this causes all kinds of hang-ups and problems in an individual's life.

You have all known great fighters in the world of boxing who were constant winners, but were flowing against the universe causing ego to become the control factor in the mental dimension. And because of this they got on an ego trip and the whole world was against them. You have also known great fighters who because they were flowing with the universe, keeping ego and imagination in their dimensions, became world heros.

You see, ego is that part of the total personality
which compares the self to other things, and when
ego gets involved in the mental dimension it causes
that individual to compare his being with other
individuals. This causes an individual to judge and
drag other people down and he never realizes that
when he is dragging somebody else down he must be
beneath them. You cannot drag somebody down if you
are above them.

To help you distinguish the fine, thin line that
separates the dimensions you might think of it in this
manner; Ego in the physical dimension tends to say, "I
can do better than you." Ego in the mental dimension
says, "I **am** better than you." Do you see the
difference? One is comparison in the physical
dimension; the other is comparison in the non-
physical dimension.

When you are going against the flow of the universe
and you get ego involved in the mental dimension,
you create worry, fear, and guilt, three of the most
destructive forces in the universe. You will seldom
experience worry, fear, or guilt except that you get
your ego involved in the mental dimension. The
reason worry and fear are such destructive forces is
because they actually undermine the legs of the
foundation of your triune. Let's say that you have
experienced a tremendous amount of positive growth
in the physical dimension, and because of this you
have many physical, material things. You also have
perfect physical health. Then you let ego get involved
in the mental dimension. You begin to worry about
the stability of the economy, when and what to buy
and sell, and sure enough, your worry causes poor

judgment. You buy and sell at the wrong time and you lose everything you have. Then you begin to worry about your health and you begin to fear illness. You fear cancer: you fear a heart attack; and sure enough, you end up having a heart attack or you end up having cancer, and by this you destroy a great amount of the growth you've experienced in the physical dimension.

Maybe you also had tremendous growth in the mental dimension. You have developed your mind; you are a good thinker; you have a good education; you have an uninhibited imagination; you are constantly experiencing new ideas. Then you begin to worry about the way you think. You realize that you think differently than most people. Then you begin to fear that other people will think you are wrong, other people will call you crazy for thinking the way you do and before very long, ego, controlling the mental dimension, creating worry and fear, undermines the mental foundation of your triune and you end up giving up your individuality.

Probably the most destructive result of getting ego involved in the mental dimension is that it stops the expression of love in that dimension. When you are on an ego trip there are very few things in the world, other than yourself, that are O.K. When you are O.K. but nothing else is, you stop your expression of love.

For thousands of years most people have been going against the flow of the universe and therefore experiencing the destruction of the ego involved in the mental dimension. If you will turn your whole thinking process around and flow with the universe from being into doing into having, naturally keeping ego in the physical dimension, you will eliminate the majority of your worry, fear, guilt, and judgment.

Physical Space ◄─────────── Mental Space ◄─────────── Spiritual Space

To keep the control factors in their correct dimensions you need to tune into your perfect space in each dimension; spiritual space, mental space, and physical space. Whether or not you are aware of it there is an innate guidance factor that is always with you or in you. You may give it any label you want to according to your belief system but it is always there and it is always striving to guide you into your perfect space. When you are going against the flow of the universe your guidance factor can only help you in the physical dimension because that's the dimension you are focused on. You block it out of the mental and spiritual dimensions. Because you are least powerful in the physical dimension, it is very easy for your guidance factor to direct you into your physical space. However, if you want to be guided to do what you are supposed to be doing and be what you are supposed to be in that space, then you should start flowing with the universe.

Because you are least powerful in the physical dimension, it was very easy for your guidance factor to direct you in the physical dimension and cause you to be physically holding this book. This does not mean that your husband or your wife or one of your friends is your guidance factor because they gave this book to you and you are reading it simply to get them off your back. If that should be the case, it simply means that you were so stubborn your guidance factor had to work through them to get you into the physical space you are occupying right now.

Now, even though your guidance factor has got you into this perfect space, if you are going against the flow of the universe, there is no way guidance can cause you to do what you are sitting here to do. Because the mental dimension is more powerful than the physical dimension you have more control over what you think about. Therefore, your guidance factor is less able to direct your thinking. Even though it may be relatively easy for your guidance factor to get you to read this book, if you are going against the flow of the universe, it may be impossible for your guidance to cause you to think what you are supposed to think while you are reading it.

Let's put this comparison in the physical level since that is where most people seem to be focused and maybe we will grasp it a little better. Let's say that I am your guidance factor and to keep this in context with most belief systems, let's also say that you cannot physically see me. Now if reading this book is your perfect physical space, it wouldn't be very difficult for me as your guide to get you to do it, whether you want to or not. I could tell some of your friends or family about the book and they might get excited about it and encourage you to read the book. I could probably even get one of them to give the book to you. If you were still resisting, I could get some of my friends to physically tie you up in the space you are in and put the book in your hands so you could start reading it.

If you are going against the universe, it is absolutely impossible for me to guide you in the spiritual dimension and cause you to be aware of how this book relates to your future possibilities. Understand that because you are more powerful in the mental dimension and most powerful in the spiritual dimension, you have more power to block your guidance in those dimensions.

If you are flowing against the universe, there is not much I can do to guide you in the mental dimension. It is nearly impossible for me to make you use your imagination and awareness and think thoughts about material you are reading.

If you are going against the universe from having into doing into being, from the physical into the mental into the spiritual, then you are also trying to go from your physical space into your mental space, and you think your physical environment causes your mental attitude. This forces your ego into your mental space and causes you to spend nearly all the time in the mental space that you are in now thinking about your next physical space, instead of thinking about what you are supposed to be doing in the physical space you are now in. However, you will never get into your next physical space until you have done what you are supposed to be doing in the space you are in right now. Your guidance factor can get you into the physical space that you are in right now with this book in front of you, but if you are flowing against the universe, it cannot cause you to think what you are supposed to think or do what you are supposed to do with the book. And you will be guided back again and again into the same physical space until you have done all of the things that you are here right now to do.

As an example, perhaps one of your next physical spaces will be in bed sleeping. If while you are reading this book you are thinking thoughts like: "I am sure getting sleepy...I'm so tired I don't understand what I'm reading...My bed is sure going to feel good tonight," then you are not doing what you are in this space to do. Do you understand? If you spend all of your time in the space you are in thinking about your next space, then you are going to have to come back and occupy this space again, or, in other words, read this book again until you have done what you are supposed to be doing in the space you are in. You see, your guidance factor will always guide you into a perfect physical space and you are going to stay in that space until you have done what you are in that space to do. If you are always thinking about your next physical space instead of doing what you are supposed to be doing in the space you are in, then you may have to stay in that space so long that it could be a very boring, tiring, unhappy, uncomfortable experience.

Let me share with you a personal experience. As a teenager I gave my life to a greater power than myself and as I look back on my life I can see how perfectly I have been guided since that time into the space that I am occupying at this moment. I can look back and see how every physical space, every home I lived in, every city, every school I attended, every job I worked at, I can see how each one of these spaces led to the next space until right now at this moment I am writing this book. However, now that I understand which direction the universe flows, I can look back and see physical spaces I occupied that were very uncomfortable, unhappy spaces. As I look back on these spaces, knowing now which direction the universe flows, I realize that I could have done everything I was supposed to do in those spaces in half the time; but since I was going against the universe, I spend the greater part of the time in many of those spaces always mentally thinking about my next physical space. In other words, I spent most of my time thinking about what I would do when I was rich, what I would do when I had a new home and a new car, what I would do when I had my own business. I spent most of my time thinking about my next physical space instead of doing what I was in that physical space to do.

Do you understand why we said earlier that if you are flowing with the universe you do not experience worry, fear, and guilt? If you are flowing with the universe, then you know that you are always doing what you are supposed to be doing and, therefore, no matter what it is, you do not need to worry.

Your guidance factor directs you through the control factor of awareness in all three dimensions.

To tune into guidance in the spiritual dimension you must tune into being. Develop an awareness of what you are being in any given moment. Are you being happy, depressed, successful, rich, patient, ill? To get to where you want to go, it is very important to know where you are now. If you know what you are being now then it is easier to change and be something different if you desire. To be guided in what you desire to be, go within yourself (techniques for this are taught in the ALPHA AWARENESS TRAINING BOOK) and simply let yourself experience a desire to be, and suddenly you will have an ah-hah that will say,

"I know what I desire to be."

If you desire to be happy, then talk intimately with yourself a few minutes about being happy. Then be still and be aware of the experience of being happy for a few minutes. Understand--you do not need to **have or do** anything to **be** happy. You can just simply be happy. You have probably experienced this a few times in your life. Haven't you at sometime in your life said, "I don't know why I feel so happy when I don't really have anything to be happy about." During those few moments of being happy without having anything to be happy about, you were flowing with the universe and you probably stopped flowing and stopped being happy the moment you thought you didn't have anything to be happy about. If you desire to be successful, go within and talk intimately with yourself about success a few minutes, and then be still and be aware of the experience of being successful for a few minutes. If you want to be an artist, intimately talk with yourself about painting. Then be still and be aware of the experience of painting a picture. You tune into your spiritual space by tuning into being. You do it by becoming aware of the things in life you deeply desire to be and then being those things.

If you will really get into your spiritual space by being aware of what you are being and then being what you truly desire to be, then it's very natural for your guidance factor to guide you in your mental space. For instance, if in the spiritual dimension you are in a state of being successful, of feeling successful, this will naturally cause you to think successful thoughts and be aware of successful ideas in the mental dimension. To be totally guided in your mental space, look at your ideas from many different perspectives. Then through the process of association and evaluation it is only natural for you to make successful decisions. Then as you flow with the universe on into your physical space, all you need to do to be guided is act. Start acting out the decisions you have made. The result is, you will have success.

As you begin to flow with the universe in your perfect space spiritually, mentally and physically be aware. Remember that your guidance comes through awareness in all three dimensions.

It is very easy to tune into your guidance factor through awareness in the physical dimension. If you are uncomfortable in the physical space you are in, it is usually because you are not being what you are supposed to be or you are not doing what you are supposed to do in the space you are in. If you are uncomfortable on your job, become aware of what you are being and doing. Are you being what your job title is, or are you being lazy or grouchy or impatient or something else that is not a part of your job? Are you doing what your job description calls for, or are you complaining or daydreaming or procrastinating or something else that is not a part of your job description? Any time you are uncomfortable, ask yourself, "Am I being and doing what I am in this space to be and do?" If you are uncomfortable in your marriage, are you being and doing what you agreed to in your marriage vows? Or are you being critical, angry, unhappy, indifferent? Are you doing a lot of complaining, quarreling, judging? A marriage vow describes being faithful and loving, honoring and supporting each other.

As you develop a greater awareness of what you are being and doing, you will find there is always a perfect physical space for you to occupy. You may demonstrate this by programming vacant parking spaces for yourself. Before you start driving, close your eyes and vividly imagine parking in the exact space you desire at your destination. It may amaze you that more than ninety-five percent of the time that particular space will be vacant for you, even in the busiest part of town. If you become aware of your perfect space and it seems as though somebody else is in it, such as somebody taking your parking space just as you are about to pull into it, realize that there is a very small percentage of the time when somebody else has a greater need of that space than you do. And if that is the case, readily and willingly give the space to them. For instance, maybe you are going to visit a friend in the hospital and you have programmed your parking space right near the entrance, and just as you are about to pull in, a car whizzes past you and takes the space. Willingly give it to them. You will probably find out it is an emergency--maybe someone who had an accident of some kind or a husband whose wife is about to have a baby in the front seat of the car. They have greater need of that space than you do.

If you are flowing with the universe and you become aware of being uncomfortable in the space that you are occupying, look around you, you may see somebody else being left out of the conversation. As you move over to give them part of your space to enter into the conversation, you become comfortable. Or maybe you look around you and you are attracted to another individual in a different space. Go over to that individual and open up a conversation and you'll find out that you are comfortable in that space, and you are giving or receiving information that is of value to you or to the other person.

One of the most important things that you can do to flow with your guidance from being into doing into having is making up fifteen to twenty Results Outlines (example, **page 64**). If you will make up fifteen to twenty Results Outlines, you will understand the simplicity of life. No matter how many outlines you make up of things you desire to be, you will almost always find the same fifteen to twenty words under "Would Be." Eventually you will grasp the ah-hah that all you need to do to accomplish anything you desire in life is to constantly be those fifteen or twenty things on your "Would Be" list. Because this is so important for your guidance, I have placed a blank Results Outline on **page 171** which I encourage you to xerox (twenty to thirty copies) and during the next few weeks, fill them out with those things you desire to be.

To help you be guided into your perfect space in all three dimensions, you may also use the affirmation of the law of release and attraction--

I release from me all (personal list) which are not a part of the perfect divine pattern of my life.

All (personal list) which are not a part of the perfect divine pattern of my life, release me.

I attract to me all (personal list) which are a part of the perfect divine pattern of my life.

All (personal list) which are a part of the perfect divine pattern of my life attract me to them.

This affirmation reads: I release from me all, and then in parentheses, personal list. In this place you will insert your own personal list of all the things you desire to release and then it continues: Which are not a part of the perfect divine pattern of my life. For instance, your list might read something like: "I release from me all people, ideas, thoughts, things, habits, emotions, words, anything which is not a part of the perfect divine pattern of my life." And then you will reverse this and say, "all people, ideas, thoughts, things, habits, emotions, words, which are not a part of the perfect divine pattern of my life, release me." You use the law of attraction in the same manner. "I attract to me all," and then include your personal list, such as "all people, ideas, thoughts, things, habits, emotions, words, which are a part of the perfect divine pattern of my life." And then, "all people, thoughts, things, ideas, habits, emotions, which are a part of the perfect divine pattern of my life, attract me to them." To use these laws of release and attraction simply go over this affirmation in your mind once or twice a day, including your personal list into it.

I do not encourage you to use this affirmation unless you are willing to let the perfect divine pattern of your life unfold. In other words, as you start using the law of release and attraction, there will be certain things in your life that will disappear that you may think you want to keep and certain things coming into your life that you may not think you want. Many years ago, Kay and I started using this affirmation of the law of release and attraction. At that time we were playing pinochle with a favorite couple of ours two to four nights a week. This was my favorite hobby at the time and I certainly didn't think I wanted to give it up. Within a week of the time we started using this affirmation, this couple disappeared from our lives and we have never seen them since. There was no argument, there was no quarrel, we just never saw them again. We lived in the same town for two more years, only about twenty blocks from them, and yet we still never saw them. When we look back on our lives, though, we realize that a lot of beautiful experiences have taken the place of the pinochle games. If it had not been for some of those experiences that replaced pinochle, I wouldn't yet be in the space I am today.

When using the law of release and attraction, you've got to be willing to mentally let go of whatever starts to disappear. Too many times when people start using this law, the minute something starts to disappear they reach out and jerk it back into their lives and, therefore, they never create the vacuum* to attract something new into their lives.

Do not make the mistake that I did when my pinochle friends disappeared from my life. I called them on the phone twenty or thirty times but the line was always busy or there was no answer. I even drove to their home several times but never found them in. When you are using the law of release and something disappears out of your life, don't waste your time trying to bring it back in.

Also be willing to accept what you are attracting into your life. Soon after I started using the affirmation of attraction, I was sitting at the counter in a restaurant having coffee and an ancient old man with a filthy hat

*Refer to ALPHA AWARENESS TRAINING BOOK

and a scraggly beard, stained with tobacco juice, sat down beside me. He made some comment about the weather and I mumbled an answer and slightly turned away from him, which terminated the conversation. Three days later on the other side of town in a different restaurant, the same filthy old man sat down beside me and attempted to start a conversation. Again, I ignored him and the conversation terminated.

Several days later in still another restaurant, the same old man sat down at the counter beside me. I finally got the ah-hah. Maybe we were being attracted to each other through my using the law of attraction. This time I opened up the conversation and got acquainted and he eventually became one of my greatest teachers. He was 87 years old and had studied metaphysics and philosophy with many of the great teachers during the beginning of this century and, to my amazement, I found my time spent with him even more exciting than playing pinochle.

If you are going to use the law of attraction, don't be as stubborn as I was. Be willing to look at the new things that you attract into your life.

I encourage you to use Alpha Awareness Training and go into the inner-conscious mind* often and ask your inner-self what are some of the ideas, attitudes, philosophies, and habits that you are hanging onto that you should release. We think of antiques as being material things in antique stores, but, believe me, we all have enough antique attitudes and philosophies to fill a dozen antique stores; thoughts and ideas that should have been put on the antique shelf years ago.

*Refer to ALPHA AWARENESS TRAINING BOOK

Understand that hanging onto an idea or attitude that may have been perfect for you ten years ago or even last week may be keeping you from your next space today. If a newly married couple continue to hang onto the attitudes and habits of a single person, their marriage probably won't last. Also be willing to look at any new philosophies or concepts or ideas that are attracted to you through books, conversations, classes or any other means.

When using the law of release and attraction please don't be concerned that you may release something from your life or attract something into your life that's not perfect for your husband or wife or someone else in your life. Understand the same guidance factor that is guiding you is also guiding eveyone else.

An even more important concept in using the law of release is releasing those things that you want to remain in your life. Circle with this concept until you grasp the enlightening ah-hah that when you release something, you no longer possess it. You no longer hold onto it. When you must hold onto things to keep them in your life, they are not really yours anyway. The best way to use the law of release in this manner is to focus upon whatever you are releasing and then say to yourself, "I release it, with love I let it go." and in your mind let that thing float into the distance to either remain there or disappear. I encourage you to use this release with all things that you *hold* dear to yourself, such as family, friends, money, your home, and so on.(There is an exercise in the ALPHA AWARENESS TRAINING BOOK specifically designed for this).

I especially encourage you to release your husband or wife. When I encourage couples to do this, many times the wife will say, "But I don't want to lose him, I just want to get along with him." But remember, the opposite of release is possession. If you release something, you no longer possess it. Now, does anyone like to be possessed? No! A lot more marriages have been destroyed because of possession than will ever be destroyed because of release, but the beautiful thing about the law of release in relation to your loved ones is that it becomes a paradox; total release becomes total possession. My lovely wife, Kay, totally possesses me because she totally releases me. And I totally possess her because every day I totally release her. This paradox sounds confusing but is very simple. If something does not possess you in any manner then there is no need to get away from it. Kay and I do not possess, hang on, or own each other in any of the three dimensions. Therefore, there is nothing we need to escape, get away from or be free of in our relationship.

The law of release is especially important in relation to parents and children. Many times we see a young son leave home. He gets married, gets a job, and becomes successful. Then he ends up failing miserably because his parents didn't release him and he didn't release his parents. His mother continues to meddle in his marriage and his family and his father interferes in business affairs, and with all the interference, his marriage breaks up and the business goes down the drain. That is why it is so important to state the law of release in both ways. In other words, you release your parents and your parents release you. Again you will see the paradox. You will find that your parents can spend even more time with you but your mother does not interfere with your marriage and father doesn't tell you how to run your business.

(Physical)   (Mental)   (Spiritual)

Action ◄———————Association · Evaluation - Decision ◄——————— Creation

It will help you tune into your perfect space if you understand that what we call creating or creation already exists in the spiritual dimension. All of the new ideas, new thoughts, inventions, books, compositions, all of your acts have their being in the spiritual dimension.

Before you can complete any creation in the physical dimension you must be aware of it from its beginning to its end. You can only create physically that which you become aware of mentally. That which you become aware of mentally already exists in the non-physical spiritual dimension. If a woman is going to make a new dress from a pattern that has never been made before she must first become aware of the idea of a new dress. Then, before she can complete the dress physically, she must become aware of every part of the pattern mentally. She can only create physically those parts of the pattern which she has already become aware of mentally. Understand that before she could possibly make the dress she had to create it from beginning to end in her mind. Therefore, the dress already existed from beginning to end before she ever started physically creating it.

This is true of all creation including the universe. Before the Creator could begin creating a physical universe, he had to be aware of it from its beginning to its end, from the Alpha to the Omega. Just like you had to see the dress from beginning to end before it could exist physically, so did the Creator have to see the universe from the beginning to the end. In other words, everything that has been, everything that is, and everything that ever will be, already was in the beginning. Everything that ever will **be** already exists in the mind of the Creator. Now this may be disturbing in that it indicates an end and yet it is true that every physical creation must have an end before it can begin. However, while you are forming the creation in your mind, you can put a new beginning in its form before it ends.

Let's say a man has the idea of creating a new kind of restaurant but he wants his restaurant to last forever, for eternity. First he imagines building his restaurant and developing it into a fine business. Then he imagines recreating a part of himself in his own image. In other words, he imagines having children. Then he imagines teaching his children every part of the business from the construction of the building to the preparation of the food to the managing of the business. He imagines that some of the children will learn the business so well they will be able to keep running his original business and teach their children to do the same. Some of his children might learn it so well that they can go out and build a chain of restaurants. And thus, the original creation may be continued or recreated into eternity because it all existed in the beginning.

In a non-tangible, non-physical form, every possible probability that may ever happen already exists;

therefore, in the non-physical spiritual dimension it is already a reality. When we human beings become aware of one of these possible probabilities that already exist in the spiritual dimension, we say that we have had a new thought or a new idea. We then bring this idea into the mental dimension and with our imagination we associate this new probability with all previously known information that might relate to it. Then, with our imagination, we evaluate the information and arrive at a decision.

To allow yourself to be guided into the most perfect decision you must look at this probability in the mental dimension from several different perspectives. From each different perspective you look at the probability. You will be able to make a different decision and each different decision would result in a different action in the physical dimension. If you will view the probability from many different perspectives in your mind, arriving at many different decisions, suddenly your awareness functioning with imagination in the mental dimension says, "Ah-hah, this is the best decision." Once you have become aware of the best decision then you take the probability on into the physical dimension and through the control factor of ego you act upon that decision. That action then results in a new act you put on or a new physical product for the scene you are acting in.

(Physical)	(Mental)	(Spiritual)
Result ◄	Effect ◄	Cause

To really flow with the universe and allow your guidance factor to direct you in making the best decisions you need a thorough understanding of the law of cause and effect.

Most people think that cause is something that happens in the physical dimension, which in turn causes some effect in what you think, do, and feel. You see, it is because we are going against the flow of the universe that we think we cause happiness. We put on some act in the physical dimension like buying a new dress or suit or car or getting high on alcohol or pot and we think that act causes us to feel happy and we feel like we have created happiness. Understand that happiness already exists. Happiness was created in the beginning, it is now and it will be in the end. Happiness is all around you, it is in you, it is going through you, it permeates the universe. Simply be aware that happiness already is and start being happy. You don't need to have anything, you don't need to do anything to be happy. When you are aware of the direction the universe flows, you simply start being happy and this will cause you to think happy thoughts in the mental dimension and result in having happiness in the physical dimension. As I mentioned before, you have probably experienced this. At one time or another haven't you said to yourself, "I don't know why I feel so happy when I don't have anything to be happy about." At that moment you were flowing with the universe and the moment you realized you didn't have anything to be happy about, you probably stopped flowing and stopped being happy.

Cause is a state of **being.** What you are being in any given moment is usually the determining factor in what you talk to yourself about. It is through your self-talk that you associate, evaluate, and arrive at decisions. Your decisions are the effect caused by your state of being. When you act upon your decision you have a result. So there is **cause, effect** and **result.** Cause is in the spiritual dimension, a state of being. Effect is in the mental dimension. a decision. Result is in the physical dimension, an action. That which already is, is the cause. Your decision is the effect of that cause and your act is the result of that effect.

From an act you will receive recogniton. If the recognition is agreement, it usually reinforces your state of being until it becomes a habit. If you are being successful, it causes you to talk to yourself about success and make effective, successful decisions. When you put your effective decisions into action, it results in your having success. From this act you receive recognition from yourself and other people. If the recognition is agreement, people saying things like, "I respect your decisions because you are always successful," it reinforces your state of being successful until finally it becomes an automatic habit.

Any cause or state of being may create different possible effects. What you are being causes the way you talk to yourself. For instance, you may experience a state of being tired. First understand you did not create the tiredness. Tiredness was in the beginning, it is now, and it will be in the end. You are simply becoming aware of being tired and that state of being is cause. At one time you may say with your self-talk (the effect), "I'm so tired, I can't stay awake," and the result in the physical dimension is you will go to sleep. At another time with your self-talk (effect) you may say, "I'm so tired I can't go to sleep," and the result will be staying awake. So the same cause can have two entirely different results depending upon the effect. If you are aware of what you are being and aware of your self-talk, then through the process of association and evaluation you can examine any thing or situation from many different perspectives. Each different perspective will allow you to see a different possible decision (effect). Then you have the freedom to choose the decision which will give you the result you desire. If you are not aware of your self-talk, then you do not have the freedom to choose the decision which will give you the result you desire. So that you may have this freedom, we will discuss self-talk in detail.

In the beginning of this book we realized we talk to ourselves every moment of our waking hours. This self-talk creates our self-confidence and most people will agree that they can accomplish anything if they are absolutely self-confident.

It has been stated by medical scientists that "the strength of any muscle in your body depends upon the confidence with which you use it." That is really a profound statement, isn't it? This is how many medical scientists explain an individual coming upon an auto accident and lifting a ton of metal off somebody pinned beneath the automobile. And yet, like so many great statements, after we have heard it a few times we end up saying, "Well, it sounds great but, so what, how does it apply to me and my situation?" Well, let's mull over and mentally digest it because this statement applies to everyone, because everyone talks to himself and self-talk creates the effect.

First, let's define confidence. There are several

definitions for confidence, but a very apt definition for understanding self-confidence might be the one: "Confidence is to intimately converse with." In other words, if you have confidence in someone, you can intimately converse with them. So then a definition of self-confidence is intimately talking with yourself. Self-confidence is your self-talk which is going on every minute of your waking hours. Hang onto this now until you mentally grasp it because, you see, this means you are self-confident of everything you do every minute you are awake. Maybe you've made the statement about someone, "They have a lot of self-confidence." Well, everyone has a lot of self-confidence.

Do you understand there is no such thing as lack of self-confidence? There isn't even any single word in the dictionary which defines lack of self-confidence. It is simply that you are self-confident of your ability to fail or you are self-confident of your ability to succeed, because, whichever one you are doing, you are intimatley talking with yourself about it and your self-talk is self-confidence. If you are intimately talking with yourself about depression, you are being absolutely self-confident about being depressed. If you are talking with yourself about illness, you are being absolutely self-confident of being ill, and didn't we already agree if you are absolutely self-confident about something you can accomplish it.

Let's put this into a comparison that you might identify with and, perhaps, that will cause you to begin intimately conversing with yourself about self-confidence and you can begin to become self-confident that you are always self-confident.

Let's take an area where self-confidence is one of the most important factors, such as professional sports. I'm sure you are aware that when a professional, who is a constant winner, retires from any major sport, there are always several large companies willing to hire him at more than $50,000 a year doing some job which he knows nothing about. Now you have probably always thought they were buying his reputation. They could care less about his reputation. What are they paying him $50,000 to $100,000 a year for? They are paying for the intimate conversation he carries on with himself.

Let's take two professionals in sports and analyze their self-talk. Let's take a sport which many of us might have experienced, such as bowling. Now we have two professional bowlers, one who is a constant, consistent winner and one who is usually a winner but every now and then he has a day when he bowls like a beginner.

The first one, who is a consistent winner, stands up in the alley, rolls his ball down the lane and lo and behold the absolute impossible happens. The ball goes off to the side and it's a gutter ball. Now, how do you suppose he intimately talks with himself. Doesn't he say something to himself like, "Come on now, relax and settle down. You can do better than that, you're a professional bowler and this next ball is going to be a perfect strike." And then he rolls his next ball and where does it go? It goes down the lane and knocks down all ten pins.

Now, talk with yourself about this. Did the second ball, which was a strike, have anything to do with the first ball, which was a gutter ball? No. After the

gutter ball he intimately talked to himself about being
a professional bowler and when he started being a
professional bowler, he started bowling perfectly.

Grasp this! If you do, you may start controlling
yourself rather than letting your environment
control you. You see, when you get up some morning
on the wrong side of the bed, so to speak, being
depressed, you know it is going to be several hours
before you can get rid of the depression. You would
understand why it takes you several hours to get rid
of the depression if you would just listen to yourself-
talk (self-confidence). Have you ever sat on the edge
of the bed some morning, being a little depressed, and
said to yourself, "This is going to be a rotten day. I can
feel it already." When you start to take a shower you
find out someone else in the family took an extra long
shower and used up all the hot water and you say to
yourself, "I knew it. It's going to be a lousy day." And
when you put on your blouse or shirt, sure enough,
it's missing a button, and you say to yourself, "I knew
it. I never should have gotten out of bed." The reason
you have a lousy day is because you are self-confident
of having a lousy day. Do you understand that when
you get up feeling depressed whether or not you feel
depressed five minutes later has nothing to do with
being depressed in the present moment? It rather has
to do with how you intimately talk with yourself
about being depressed or not being depressed.

Most people go through life thinking what is
happening this minute or this hour largely controls
what will happen the next minute or the next hour.
But instead it is what you intimately say to yourself
this minute that will control what happens the next
minute.

Let's take our second professional bowler, the one who usually wins but every now and then has a day when he bowls like a beginner. He stands up and rolls his first ball down the lane and it, too, is a gutter ball. Now how do you suppose he talks to himself? Isn't it something like "(sigh) ..Today is going to be one of those days. You watch, I'll bowl like a beginner this whole game. I might as well quit now." Then he rolls his second ball, and where does it go? That's correct, down the side and into the gutter. Now did his first gutter ball cause him to roll the second gutter ball? No! What caused him to roll the second gutter ball was that his self-talk (self-confidence) confirmed that he was being a beginning bowler.

Let's take two amateur bowlers and compare their self-talk. The first amateur stands up, rolls his ball down the lane and it goes down the center and knocks down all ten pins. A perfect strike. Now his self-talk goes something like this, "Wow, did you see that? Boy, today's my day. You just watch. Today I'm going to bowl a perfect game." Then he rolls his second ball and where does it go? Correct! Down the center for another perfect strike. Now did his first strike cause him to roll the second strike? No! Instead it was how he talked to himself after he made the first strike that resulted in the second strike. In other words, he became totally self-confident of making another strike. His self-talk created the **effect.** The **result** was making another strike.

Then we have our second amateur bowler. He stands up and rolls his first ball down the lane and it, too, goes down the center and knocks down all ten pins. Now, his self-talk goes something like this:

"Man, I don't know how I ever did that. I'll never be able to do that again." And then he rolls his second ball and where does it go? Correct. Off to the side and down the gutter. Do you understand? His self-talk after he made the first strike was simply total self-confidence that he would not be able to make another strike.

Now, you might say, "But there are days when I talk to myself about bowling a perfect game and I expect to bowl a perfect game. I even really believe I'm going to bowl a perfect game, but I end up bowling a lousy game, so what went wrong?" To understand why this happens many times we need to go a little deeper into our self-talk because the reality is that nothing ever happens to you except that you have talked to yourself about it.

To understand this you must realize there are three levels of self-talk. There is the conscious self-talk which is your subvocalization, mentally forming words into sentences but not speaking them out loud. Then there is a subconscious self-talk which is your predominant thought patterns constantly going through your mind. And then there is the unconscious self-talk which are the fleeting thoughts and images associated with the predominant thought patterns.

As we discussed earlier, your fears and worries come from your subconscious mind. If you are worried about bowling poorly, to overcome the worry you may consciously affirm to yourself, "Tonight I'm going to bowl a 200 game," but your worry causes your subconscious self-talk to say, "But I'll be happy if I make 150." And with this subconscious self-talk your unconscious self-talk may flash an image of a gutter ball so rapidly that you are not even aware of it.

Circle with this concept until you grasp it and you may understand why your positive thinking, metaphysics, positive mental attitude, and other related concepts do not always work for you. Many times your affirmations do not work for you because you are affirming them in your conscious mind and then because of worry, fear, or doubt, you are cancelling them out in your subconscious mind.

If you are concerned about a particular test, you may affirm in your conscious self-talk, "I am going to make an 'A' on my history test today," and then your concern or doubt causes your subconscious self-talk to flash the message, "But I'll settle for a 'C'." And you nearly always end up with the results of the subconscious self-talk rather than the conscious self-talk. (The ALPHA AWARENESS TRAINING BOOK has exercises that will teach you how to control your subconscious and unconscious self-talk.)

It is easier to change what you are being from negative to positive if you are aware of your self-talk. Understand that you may use your self-talk (self-confidence) to reinforce what you are being or to make you aware of a different state of being. As you develop an awareness of what you are being in any given moment, then it becomes easier to flow with the universe and control your state of being in a positive manner.

What you are being **causes** your self-talk and decisions which are an **effect.** When you put your decision into action, that is the **result.** Change what you are being and you automatically change your self-talk.

When you are going against the flow of the universe you think that having money causes you to own your new house or to travel or be rich, but as we realized earlier in the book, when you are flowing with the universe it is being rich that causes you to travel and have money and have your new home.

When you are going against the flow of the universe you are trying to use the law of cause and effect in reverse. And you may be saying things like, "How can I be successful when I have so many debts? How can I be in perfect health when I have arthritis? How can I get a new job when I don't have any experience? How can I think about owning my own businesss when I don't have an education? How can I be rich when I don't have any money? How can I be happy when I don't have anything to be happy about?" You think all things in life depend upon what you have. When you are going against the universe, you constantly have the feeling that your physical space is creating your mental space and spiritual space. When you are going against the universe, you have the feeling that your physical environment, your physical body, your clothes, your home, the cars you have, your parents or children, your friends, your enemies, your teachers, your minister, the city in which you live, cause you to be what you are. You think it is these physical things that cause you to think the way you think and feel the way you feel and be what you are. But that is not so. What you are being **causes** the **effect** of your thinking and your thinking **results** in what you have and don't have.

(Physical)   (Mental)   (Spiritual)
Results of Love ◄————————Love Expressed ◄————————Love Is

You see, in the spiritual dimension love simply is. You don't create it, you don't make it, you don't cause it. Love was in the beginning, it is now, it will be in the end. Love permeates the universe. It is around you. It is in you. You simply become aware of being love, you become aware of being O.K. Then in the mental dimension you experience the effect of love, which is the expression of love itself. The expression of love is simply granting being. Granting being to everything to be what it is and not be what it is not. Or, in other words, allowing everything and anything to be O.K., just like it is. This effect or expression of love then ends up having a result in the physical dimension. You end up having all the hugs, kisses, the affection, the sharing, the caring, the kindness, that we originally called love but which is only a result of the effect of love in the mental dimension which was caused by an awareness of being love in the spiritual dimension.

You will have found a new freedom in life if you simply understand that what you have in the physical world is the result of what you do in the mental dimension. And what you do in the mental world is the effect of what you are being in the spiritual dimension. Understanding this will make it so much easier for you to learn new acts as you go through life and have the results and recognition that you desire.

(Physical)		(Mental)	(Spiritual)
Perform ──► Receive	Recognition ◄──	Learn Act ◄────────	Probable Acts
↓	↓		
Comfort Zone	Problem Answer		
	$20,000 or $25,000		

All of the acts you will ever learn have already been created in the spiritual dimension. Before you came on this vacation you had awareness in the spiritual dimension. You were aware of every probability that could possibly happen to you while you are on this vacation. With awareness of everything that could possibly happen to you, you still came on this trip, so you see, it really must be O.K. You may say, "But why can't I remember now, why did I have to forget?" If you totally knew where you came from, what you were doing, and who you were, why be here? It's no vacation, is it? Can you understand that there has to be some separation or this is no vacation. If you didn't forget, you would just be bringing the job with you. You must have some separation to get a new persepective when you go back to where you came from.

This intense desire to know where we came from before birth and where we are going after death creates an interesting paradox that I find somewhat amusing. And reflecting upon it certainly eliminates the frustration in my seeking and searching. The paradox is that we came here so that we could forget about who we were, where we came from, and what we were doing and then we spend all of our time here trying to figure out what it is that we came to forget.

In the other dimension we have awareness in the unconscious and subconscious areas of mind as well as the conscious area of mind. From experience it seems that the unconscious mind perceives the future, the subconscious mind perceives the past, and the conscious mind relates to the present. Being aware in all three areas of the mind in the non-physical dimension causes us to experience the "now" moment. Let's put this into an example in our physical world where we are focused so that we might better understand. In the Alpha Awareness Training there is an exercise that teaches photographic memory. When you experience photographic memory you do not think back to the experience and recall it in bits and pieces, you simply fire the total brain cell pattern as it was initially impressed and the experience seems to be happening again in the present moment. In other words, if you think about your fifth birthday, with photographic memory you will again re-experience your fifth birthday at that moment. You will see before you the cake and candles, all of the different presents and the children at the party. You will see the color of clothing and costumes. You will feel the same excitement and happiness and, in talking about it you wouldn't say, "I **had** a cake with five candles," instead, you would say, "I **have** a cake with five candles."

Now, if you had total photographic memory from the moment of your birth up to the present moment, you would have no past in this life-time. In other words, if I asked you what you did on your tenth birthday, you wouldn't talk about it as a past experience. Instead, you would say, "I am doing such and such." You would be bringing your past experience into the present moment and so you would have no past.

Now we also know that human beings, to a greater or lesser degree, have the ability to experience a future event in the present. In other words, you might experience some future event through precognition or you might simply dwell upon a future event through precognition or you might simply dwell upon a future event until you had actually experienced every probability of it in the present moment.

If we could open up our unconscious mind and perceive every possible thing that could happen to us in the future, as we can do in the past with photographic memory, then we would have no future because our future would be now. In other words, if I asked you what you would be doing five years from now, you wouldn't answer, "**I will** be doing." Instead, you would say, "**I am** doing." Total photographic memory from the moment of our birth until now, and total precognitive awareness to perceive our future to the point of death would eliminate the past and the future because we would experience them both as "now." If you were living in the now moment with the past and the future happening with the present, every now and then you might want to take a break.

You have probably had some embarrassing, awkward, unhappy experiences in your past which you have mostly forgotten about and you live very comfortably with them today because you only recall them in fragments and pieces. If you had total photographic memory, every time you thought of one of those experiences you would be reliving it again.

If on your seventeenth birthday you had borrowed your father's car and gone out to celebrate with some of your friends and on the way home had an accident which killed two of your best friends, it would have been an extremely unpleasant experience. However, years later you could live with that experience because you would only remember bits and pieces of it. If you had total photographic memory, everytime you thought of it, you would be reliving it and I'm sure that after a time you would say, "I want to forget."

You may also have some embarrassing, unhappy experiences in your future. If you had total precognitive awareness, every time you thought of one of those experiences in the future, you would be experiencing it now. And every now and then you might say, "I'd like to take a vacation and forget it for awhile."

Well, it is the experience of that now moment in the non-physical dimension that you came on this vacation to forget for awhile. In the non-physical dimension the now moment is far greater than our comparison of a now moment in this physical dimension. When you go back from this vacation, after going through a period of adjustment, you will again be aware in your conscious, subconscious and unconscious mind all at the same time. That awareness will give you so-called photographic memory of every moment of your existence, whatever it has been up to the present moment. Being aware in the unconscious mind you will also have total precognitive awareness of everything that will happen in your future as far into time as you can see your future, and at some point in what we call the future, you may again decide to get away from it all for a little while and take another vacation.

All you need to do to get away from it all is create a physical body with a brain. The brain acts as a filtering mechanism through which we perceive mind and it filters out nearly all of your unconscious awareness which perceives your future, most of your subconscious awareness which perceives your past, and allows conscious awareness of the present to come through totally.

The probability of everything that you can possibly do while on this vacation already exists in the spiritual dimension. These probabilities include all of the roles that you might act out or any of the props that you might create for the stage (planet Earth), such as inventions, paintings, books, buildings, or any of the other props that we use to act out our roles.

When you become aware of one of these probabilities, you bring that awareness into the mental dimension, and with imagination, through the process of association and evaluation, you arrive at a decision, to do it or not to do it. If your decision is to do it, then in the mental dimension you memorize that act. As you memorize the act in the mental dimension you begin performing that act in the physical world. As you perform the act it develops into a habit or a prop and in performing the act, you receive recognition or agreement. The recognition you receive then becomes a problem or an answer.

Let's say that in the spiritual dimension the probable act that you become aware of is being an accountant. And so, in the mental dimension, you make the decision to put that act into effect and you memorize the act of being an accountant. You study. You go through school. You get your degrees; until finally you are able to perform the act in the physical dimension. Before long the act of being an accountant becomes a comfort zone. From performing the act you are going to receive recognition. Let's say the recognition you're receiving for putting on the act of being an accountant is $20,000 a year which is a problem because you need $25,000 a year. Now, realize that it's not the act that is the problem, instead it is the recogniton you are receiving for the act that is the problem.

(Mental)	(Spiritual)
View Act from Different Perspectives	Awareness of Another Act

If you will keep the control factors, ego and imagination, in their proper dimensions, you may solve the problem in either the mental or spiritual dimensions. To find a solution in the mental dimension, you simply look at the act with your imagination from every possible perspective. As you are looking at the act from many different perspectives, you must be sure that ego does not get involved. If ego gets involved in the mental dimension like it does with many people, then you have a tendency to say, "The reason I have this problem is because my boss doesn't like me and he is not paying me as much as I'm worth." Instead of getting ego involved, just look at the accountant act you are putting on and the recognition you are receiving for it with pure imagination in every perspective you possibly can, and then suddenly awareness functioning with imagination says, "Ah-hah, I see a solution. I can run a few ads in the paper and get a few clients that I can do work for in the evenings. I can build this into a small part-time accounting business and that will enable me to make an additional $5,000 a year." When the new act is memorized and put into action, it becomes an answer.

You may also find a solution in the spiritual dimension by going into inner-conscious mind and becoming aware of a totally new act. Then learn the new act in the mental dimension and put it into effect and perform the new act in the physical dimension. To be aware of the new act, you simply go into inner-conscious mind and desire to be aware of a new role that you might enjoy and perform well that would give you $25,000 a year in recognition. As different roles are going through your mind you will suddenly receive an ah-hah about some particular role you desire to play. Maybe that role is selling airplanes. In the mental dimension you memorize the act of selling airplanes and then in the physical dimension you perform the act and receive your $25,000 per year in recognition.

You do not have to physically act out a role to make it real. When you memorize a role mentally it is just as real to you as if you had actually acted it out. As an example, let's say you were enrolled in drama class in high school and your class put on a play which required fifteen characters but there were only thirteen students. Because you were an excellent drama student, the teacher had you memorize three different roles--the role of the Indian, the Irishman, and the Englishman. Shortly after you memorized all three roles an Irish student enrolled in the class, so your teacher gave the Irishman's role to the new student. Then a week later an Indian student enrolled and the teacher gave this new student the Indian's role and you ended up acting out the role of the

Englishman on stage. However, you had totally memorized all three roles. Many years later if someone were to ask you which character you were in the play in drama class, you might not be able to recall. You might say you were not sure but you think it was an Irishman, or perhaps you played the part of an Indian, or maybe it was an Englishman. Anyway, you know you memorized all three. What I am saying is that any thoughts you dwell on at any length become your reality. They are just as real whether you physically act them out or not.

(Physical)	(Mental)	(Spiritual)
It is all an Act So it is all Perfect ◄	All Roll Are Perfect ◄	Probabilities are Perfect

It will certainly make it easier for you to learn new acts if you understand that all probabilities in the spiritual dimension are perfect, all ideas, all creation that exists in the spiritual dimension is perfect. There is no right or wrong in the spiritual dimension. There is no such thing as an imperfect idea, an imperfect creation, until something is done with it.

You may ask, "But what if you become aware of a very involved murder plot? Would that be perfect?" As long as it remains in the spiritual dimension it is perfect. Even while you are memorizing it in the mental dimension it is perfect. When you bring it into the physical dimension, depending on how you act it out, you might then call it perfect or imperfect. In other words, if you became aware of a very involved plot to murder your mother-in-law, and in the mental dimension you decided to write it into a murder novel and published the novel and received $100,000 for it, you probably wouldn't call that imperfect. However, if you physically acted out the plot and murdered your mother-in-law, the results may not be so desirable.

Now, if it makes sense that probabilities are perfect in the spiritual dimension, that there is no right or wrong in the spiritual dimension, then perhaps you can accept that these same roles are perfect while you are learning them in the mental dimension.

If you have followed the perfection of your act this far in the mental dimension, then perhaps you can grasp that everything you have ever done in your whole life has been perfect. Whatever you are doing right now is perfect, and whatever you will do in the future will be perfect. Let's stagger the imagination with that again. Everything you have ever done in your life has been perfect. Whatever you are doing right now is perfect, and anything that you ever do in the future will also be perfect. You see, if everything you do in the physical dimension is an act, if every moment is an act, then it all has to be perfect. You say, "But, Wally, what if you forget what you are saying while you are talking to a group. What if you stumble over your lines. Is that a perfect act?" Sure, isn't that a perfect act of forgetting my lines? Could I forget my lines any more perfectly? But then you might say, "But what if you were playing with a knife and you slipped and cut your thumb off? Would that be perfect?" Sure, wouldn't that be a perfect act of cutting off my thumb? "But," you say, "what if you only cut it halfway off?" Then wouldn't that be a perfect act of cutting my thumb off halfway? Could I cut my thumb halfway off any more perfectly? You see, it's all an act.

There is no dress rehearsal in the physical

dimension. Your only dress rehearsal is in the mental dimension through your self-talk. Every moment in the physical dimension is an act, so it is all perfect. **What is happening now is not perfect for tomorrow or next week or next year, but it is perfect for now.** You may say though, "If it is all perfect then why change? Why learn any new acts?" There is no reason to change unless you want different recognition. If you want a different kind of recognition, in other words, more money, more friends, a new home, a new car, inner peace, relaxation, happiness, enlightenment, anything that you are not experiencing now, then you must change. You must learn a new act which will result in that recognition.

(Physical)	(Mental)	(Spiritual)
Act Without Decision ◄ ————	—See Perfection ◄ ————	The Innerself - Perfect

If you understand the perfection of your acts, then perhaps you can begin acting with total freedom. To most people freedom means freedom of choice or the freedom to decide what you want to do. But that is the biggest thing in life you will ever be a slave to--your freedom of choice, your freedom to decide. Is there anything more frustrating in your life than your decisions? Should you spank the kid, should you ignore him? Should you divorce her or should you stay married? Should you order a hamburger and french fries or just a salad? Should you buy more stock or sell what you have? Is it not true that your decisions in life are your most frustrating moments? No wonder you haven't been experiencing any freedom. What you have been calling freedom is what you are being a slave to.

Total freedom has no choice. **Total freedom has no choice.** It has to be that way if decisions cause most of your frustration because frustration is not freedom. You may naturally ask, "But how can I do anything in life without making decisions?" It is possible to flow through life without making any decisions but to do so you must turn your life around and totally flow with the universe from the spiritual dimension into the mental dimension into the physical dimension. Totally flowing with the universe allows your inner guidance to tell you what to be, do and have and you no longer have to make the decisions through your conscious ego. To receive the inner guidance you need to become aware of the non-physical aspects of yourself which represent the spiritual, mental, and physical dimensions. These three aspects of your total personality are so distinct that you can actually perceive them as three separate images of yourself in your mind. In Alpha Awareness Training we refer to those images as the spiritual inner-self, mental inner-self, and physical inner-self and once you have perceived them, you can communicate with them just like you can with another person. There is a complete exercise in the ALPHA AWARENESS TRAINING BOOK for meeting your inner-selves. If you have not gone through Alpha Awareness Training or read the ALPHA AWARENESS TRAINING BOOK, you should be able to meet your inner-selves with the following exercise.

Sit down in a very comfortable position and close your eyes. Then imagine yourself completely relaxed, physically and mentally. Then imagine a state of spiritual, mental, and physical well-being, whatever that means to you as an individual. Continue with an exercise like this five or ten times until you really feel you are accomplishing a state of physical relaxation and a state of spiritual, mental and physical well-being for you as an individual. Then you may successfully go into an exercise of meeting your inner-selves. To do this, get yourself into that state of spiritual, mental and physical well-being and then do one of the following, whichever seems to work best for you:

1. You may imagine yourself standing in front of a full-length mirror and imagine your reflection in the mirror as vividly as you can. Then imagine the reflection becoming lifelike, real and animated.

2. You may imagine three different reflections stepping out of the mirror becoming lifelike, real and animated.

3. You may imagine the mirror dissolving and dissipating and the reflection remaining lifelike, real and animated.

4. You may find it works better for you to imagine yourself stepping into the mirror and meeting your inner-self.

Then simply become acquainted with this image of yourself as you would any person you might meet.

You might begin by shaking hands and asking, "Who are you? Who am I? How can I help you? How can you help me?" You may have to do the exercise several times before you perceive all three images. When you have perceived all three images at the same time, it will be very clear to you which one represents the spiritual dimension, mental dimension, and physical dimension. When you have developed the exercise so you are able to communicate with your spiritual inner-self it's very apparent that that part of you is perfect and beautiful. That part of you is loving and lovable. That part of you is love. It is not necessary that you see images of your spiritual, mental and physical inner-selves. However it is necessary to work with this concept until you can feel an aspect of yourself that is spiritual, that is peace, love and perfection, that part of yourself that is the source of your inner peace and love.

To act with freedom without decision you simply become aware of that part of yourself which is love and perfection and then see the same perfection in the other person or the problem and then simply act without making a decision.

Let's say you are grocery shopping with your three-year-old and because you will not buy him a forty dollar toy he wants, he throws a temper tantrum in the main aisle in the grocery store. He starts screaming, yelling, beating his fists and banging his head on the floor. Now, what do you do? You get to experience what you've been calling freedom, making a decision. Should you spank him, should you ignore him, should you walk off and pretend he's not yours and forget him? Should you pick him up and love him, what should you do? That's what you have been calling freedom; the necessity of making a decision.

If you want to experience total freedom at that moment, then experience your inner-self, the real you inside, as love and perfection. Then look at the child and look through the act of a temper tantrum he is putting on and see the same love and perfection within the child. See in him what he is and not how he is acting. When you are experiencing yourself as love and perfection and the child as love and perfection, then start acting. Don't stop and decide what to do, just simply act, whatever act starts taking place, but without decision. You see, if you are experiencing your love and perfection and the child's love and perfection, what can come from that except more love and perfection? It simply means that whatever act you start doing in that moment has to be the most perfect act that can take place in that moment. If you have a jar filled with water, what can you pour out of the jar except water? If you are experiencing only perfection, what can come from that except more perfection. While you are experiencing perfection, act without decision. It does not matter if you spank him or walk off and ignore him. Whatever you end up doing without decision in that moment will be the most perfect thing that can be done.

When you experience an ah-hah, you do not think of it as a decision, do you? When you experience an ah-hah there is no debate going on in your mind. An ah-hah is simply knowing. If someone asks you what 2+2 is, you don't decide that the answer if 4, you simply know the answer is 4. That is the way an ah-hah is. It is simply knowing.

You have acted without making a decision many times in many ways during your life. One way common to many people is acting out of anger. Possibly at some time in your life you have been aware of your anger and another person's anger at the same time and then spontaneously acted without a decision. This happens many times between parents and children and husbands and wives. If the act is coming from anger, it will create more anger. If the act is coming from love, it will create more love. If the act is coming from perfection, it will create more perfection.

If your action to the temper tantrum is based on a decision, understand what you decide has very little to do with the present tantrum but, instead, is primarily based on what? Yes, previous like information. Through the process of association and evaluation, your decision is based on previous temper tantrums. What your doctor says to do about temper tantrums, what your mother would do, or what she did to you when you were three years old. Part of your decision may be based on what you think the people in the grocery store think you should do. Now, making a decision in this manner is O.K. It's just that you usually experience frustration instead of freedom. When you experience yourself as perfection and you see the perfection in the problem, in other words, allow it to be O.K., then the action comes as an "ah-hah." There is no mental debate; you simply know how to act.

(Physical)	(Mental)	(Spiritual)
Inner-Self Audience ◄ ————	Inner-Self Director ◄ ————	Inner-Self – Agent

To act with total freedom you need to know thyself. Some twenty six hundred years ago a man said the greatest wisdom in the world is to know thyself. This statement has never been debated by a wise man since. As you become acquainted with who you are and what you are inside of your costume, you can truly experience the kingdom within because that kingdom is within your reality right now. All you need to do to experience that inner kingdom is to get into your inner-conscious mind and become totally acquainted with your inner-selves. When you can distinguish and communicate with all three aspects of yourself, then consider your physical body to be an actor on stage and allow your spiritual inner-self to act as your agent deciding what roles and characters you will act out. Allow your mental inner-self to be your director, telling you how to act out the roles to get the recognition you desire. And allow your physical inner-self to be your audience, giving you recognition for the act you're putting on. To accomplish this, you must reverse your life and totally flow with the universe. When you are going against the flow of the universe, your ego, representing your physical inner-self, is always acting as your director and agent even though it is not qualified for the job.

To understand this flow it is not necessary that you see images of your spiritual, mental and physical inner-selves. However, it is necessary to work with this concept until you can feel an aspect of yourself that is spiritual, that is peace, love and perfection, that part of yourself that is the source of your inner peace and love. And then feel another aspect of yourself which represents the mental dimension that you may think of as the intellect which is capable of carrying out the directions. The third aspect of yourself representing the physical dimension you will probably recognize as ego, that part of you that has been constantly comparing you to your environment and judging you and the things in the environment to be right or wrong.

When you are going against the flow of the universe,

ego takes over in all three dimensions and is always acting as your director and agent even though it is not qualified for the job. Since ego comes from the least powerful dimension (the physical) and is not qualified to guide you in the mental or spiritual dimensions, it constantly feels insecure and threatened by the mental and spiritual dimensions. Because it is insecure and threatened, it instantly judges anything that seems to disagree with it as wrong including the mental and spiritual aspects of yourself.

You have probably known someone who has been promoted to a job or position for which they are not qualified. And being insecure, they feel like any suggestion for change is a personal criticism making them wrong and so they are constantly attacking everyone else's ideas. In this same manner, when you are going against the flow of the universe, you automatically promote your ego to the position of director and agent and it constantly attacks ideas from your spiritual and mental inner-selves.

Since ego is only concerned with having, when you are going against the flow, ego strives to make you think that all causes are physical instead of spiritual. It is the ego acting as your director and agent that makes you think you must **have** something to be happy about.

If you will flow with the universe you eliminate the need for judgment and, therefore, eliminate the need for ego. When you eliminate the need for ego, you eliminate your need for other actresses' and actors' agreement as your audience and your physical inner-self automatically takes the place of ego and becomes your audience and, without judgment, always applauds you for a perfect act. In other words, it applauds you for cutting your thumb off perfectly or cutting your thumb halfway off perfectly or not cutting your thumb at all perfectly.

When you start flowing totally with the universe, your ego may violently resist. The easiest way to eliminate this resistance is to apply the O.K. concept in place of judging something as right or wrong. Eliminating the need for ego in this manner is the answer you've always been looking for. You have gone through life always wanting to be, do and have the right thing without going through the agonizing process of making the right decision. If you are totally flowing with the universe, your spiritual self will automatically guide you into being that which is perfect for you. This then creates self-talk in the mental dimension which is a natural effect of what you are being and so there is no conflict creating a need for decision in what to do or how to do it in the physical dimension.

Perhaps it would be easier to put this concept in perspective if you the reader will, at this time, vividly imagine yourself as being one of two hundred students attending an Alpha Awareness Results Seminar and I, Wally Minto, the author, am standing in front of the class delivering the lecture. If you vividly imagine yourself to be in this situation, then it is pretty easy to get the perspective that I am an actor up front putting on an act and you are the audience. It's even pretty easy to get the perspective that you are actors putting on an act and I am your audience.

But let's go a step further. Let's imagine all of our physical inner-selves coming out of us and sitting up in the balcony looking down and watching this stage show going on right now called an Alpha Awareness Results Seminar on "How to Flow with the Universe." Now who is the audience? The inner-selves are now the audience. If our inner-selves are the audience, then we become the actors in this show.

Can you understand now why I do not need your agreement? You see, we are all actors in the same scene. We said before that actors do not expect applause from each other. They only expect applause from their audience. If we imagine this scene to be real, my part of the act is to stand up and act like a lecturer. Your part of the act is to act like an audience and no matter how you are acting, you are playing your part perfectly in this Alpha Awareness Results scene. In any scene like this--in a movie, on TV, or anywhere else--there have to be different roles to make the show interesting. Wouldn't it be a boring show if everybody were just sitting there listening, agreeing with everything I say? And so we have different characters playing different roles. Maybe one actor gets his cue and becomes bored and another actor on cue disagrees with what is being said. Maybe another actor plays his role by going to sleep and another by listening and understanding, and Wally plays his role by talking on and on. All the while the inner-selves are sitting up in the balcony applauding each actor and actress for playing their parts perfectly. Can you understand now why it is so easy for me to grant you being? Can you see why it is so easy for me to say you are O.K. just the way you are? Accept the class, reject the class, like me, dislike me, stay or leave, stay awake, go to sleep. Whatever you do, it's O.K. You are playing your part in the Alpha Awareness Results scene and you are playing it perfectly.

The only change we need in order to grasp this as it really is, is to realize that our inner-selves are not sitting up in the balcony. Our inner-selves are **inside** of us looking out through the costume, watching all of us actors putting on the Alpha Awareness Results scene and applauding each one of us for doing a perfect job. Understand the simplicity of Ernest Holmes' message that says, "People seek all over the world, seeking with that which they are seeking for."

Even after you understand all of this, you still carry out the garbage; you still wash the dishes and mop the floor; you still bring home the paycheck; but you sit inside watching yourself carry out the garbage and applaud yourself for putting on a perfect act of carrying out the garbage. This is freedom because you no longer have the need of other people's agreement to make you right. When you let go of that you let go of the majority of your hang-ups in your life. So tomorrow as you go through the day and you see people griping and complaining, sit back inside yourself and understand that they are just acting out the roles they have memorized. If you want more peace and love and joy in the scene, then get back inside yourself and see yourself as an actor in the whole scene and understand you have the freedom to change your lines and ad-lib at any moment you so desire.

When you start ad-libbing on stage, what do all the other actors and actresses have to do to stay in the act? They, too, must ad-lib. So tomorrow in some of your scenes--on the job, at school, or whatever it may be--why don't you do a little ad-libbing? Instead of playing your usual role using the memorized lines about aches and pains, lousy working conditions, dishonest politicians, and all of your problems, use a few different lines like: "It's a beautiful day. I feel wonderful. I feel like getting things done today." Lines such as these will naturally shock the other actors and actresses on the same stage with you. Their first reaction is to think you're crazy and call you wrong. But if you keep on ad-libbing lines such as these, eventually you will find the other actors and actresses changing their lines and getting into your new act while they are on stage with you. They, too, begin to act like it's a beautiful day and they feel wonderful.

THE TRUTH SHALL SET YOU FREE - THE TRUTH IS

In the spiritual dimension everything already is. When you become aware of something that already is, you bring it into the mental dimension and from your perspective you arrive at a decision. If your decision accepts it as it truly is, you have seen the truth of it and it will give you freedom. If your decision does not accept it as it is, you create an illusion and the illusion will enslave you.

In the spiritual dimension depression is and, therefore, you may often become aware of it. Then in the mental dimension you will make a decision about it. If in your decision you see the truth of depression, it will give you freedom. If you see the illusion, it will enslave you.

Most people see the illusion of depression and it enslaves them. Because of this, when people become depressed, the depression hangs onto them. They can't seem to get rid of it and this causes them to become more depressed. Their guilt then causes the depression to last longer and it becomes a vicious circle. People suffer through their periods of depression only because they see the illusion of depression.

I, too, go through my periods of depression but I do it on purpose. Because I learned to see the truth of depression, my depression sets me free. It gives me happiness and relaxation. It rests me and helps me accomplish more in my work.

Let me share with you an experience of my depression so you might understand this. Some time ago I arrived home from a three-week lecture tour. Three days later I was to leave again on another speaking tour. Before I arrived home I had those three days planned in infinite detail so that I could accomplish everything that needed to be done before I left again. Upon arriving home my wife told me something that had just happened which would require several hours of my time and energy. This, of course, upset my detailed plans and it seemed impossible that I would be able to accomplish everything that had to be done in the three days. With this realization I became aware of depression. In the mental dimension I decided to go ahead and start acting depressed so that I could receive the freedom and rest from the truth of depression.

Now I didn't feel that I should force the family to take part in my depression act so I told Kay she might want to take the children and go to the movies or visit someone. As soon as Kay and the children were gone I started getting into my act of depression. I started talking to myself about all the things that people expected me to do in Alpha Awareness and that Alpha Awareness students didn't understand the tremendous amount of time and energy involved in keeping the organization going. I told myself there was no way I could get all of the things done by myself. I became so depressed that I could no longer be responsible for my business. If you are totally depressed, you simply cannot be responsible for your job. So I set Alpha Awareness aside. I didn't stop there. I got deeper into depression. I talked to myself about all the money that was needed to continue the growth of Alpha Awareness Training and that it would probably be impossible to get the tremendous sums of money we need for research. I became so depressed I was no longer responsible for my financial responsibilities and so I set all financial responsibilities aside. I wallowed still deeper in depression. I became so depressed I couldn't even be responsible for my family. There I was with all of the things to be accomplished during those three days and my family didn't even care. They were downtown watching a movie. Do you understand what I was doing? I was simply taking the mental responsibilities off my shoulders and setting them aside for a few minutes. I got so deep in depression that I wasn't even morally responsible. Had I committed a crime in those few minutes and a psychiatrist could have analyzed the state of depression I was in, he certainly would have said that I was not morally responsible for my actions.

Understand, I loved every minute of this. I simply allowed my spiritual inner-self to select the role of being depressed and my mental inner-self to direct my depression act through my self talk. My physical inner-self was the audience applauding and cheering me for putting on a fantastic depression act with my body. I used the depression to set aside all of my mental and moral responsibilities for a short rest period. It is kind of like walking along carrying two five-gallon buckets of water. What do you want to do pretty soon? Sure, you want to set them down and rest. Now, after you have rested for about fifteen minutes, then what do you feel like doing? At that point you naturally feel like picking the buckets up and continuing. But how would you feel at that moment if someone told you you couldn't touch the buckets of water for two or three days, that for two or three days you must simply sit and wait before you could go on with your job? You see, setting your responsibilities aside through depression is taking a mental rest. But because many people do not see this truth in depression, they feel guilty about their depression and make it last for two or three days. After taking a forty-five minute depression break in that particular situation, I was able to accomplish everything I had planned in the three days, plus the extra work, and had time to take my wife and children out to dinner on the third evening.

In using this perspective toward depression, I find that I can only make my periods of depression last twenty minutes to an hour and I enjoy every minute of them.

You might keep this concept in mind as a formula.

The more freedom you are receiving from anything, the closer you are getting to the truth.

My friends, the truth shall set you free. The truth is you are a spiritual being, using mind to express through a physical body in a physical world, allowing a little part of you to be human. In the future, I invite you to play the game of truth. It's the most exciting game you will ever play because you always win. When you play the game of truth, you can't lose. It's like playing a slot machine, but every time you pull the handle you win. Maybe one time it is only a nickel, maybe another time it's twenty-five cents, and maybe the next time you hit the jackpot, but you always win.

As you are acting out the role of truth in the future, I would like you to know there is at least one person in the world who grants you, as an individual, total being. Whenever you are a little depressed or discouraged, think on this a moment. No matter how many hang-ups you think you have, no matter how horrible you think you are, whoever you are and wherever you are, I, for one person, really love you, because I know you are really beautiful and perfect. Even though we may have never met, I still know that you are really O.K., just the way you are.

Good health, God bless you. I really love you and I wish you a happy vacation. I grant you being.

Wally Minto

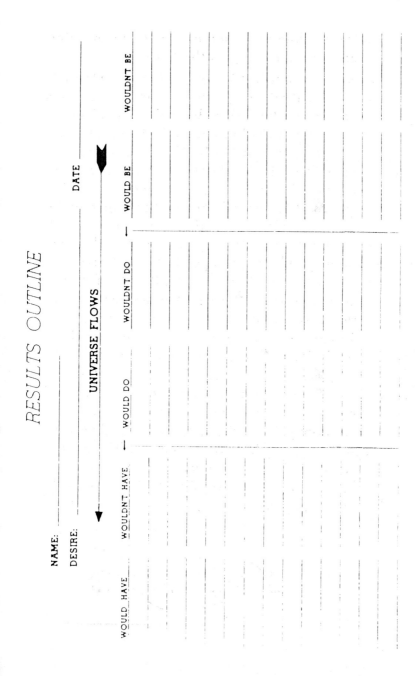

ORDER FORM

Please send me _____ Results Book (s)

I have enclosed $12.00 per book $_____

Name _____

Address _____

City _____State _____Zip _____

Phone_____
Date _____

MAIL TO:
Alpha Awareness
Drawer G
Susanville, CA 96130

ORDER FORM

Please send me _____ Results Book (s)

I have enclosed $12.00 per book $_____

Name _____

Address _____

City _____State _____Zip _____

Phone_____
Date _____

MAIL TO:
Alpha Awareness
Drawer G
Susanville, CA 96130